A GIANT'S STRENGTH   America in the 1960s

A GIANT'S STRENGTH
America in the 1960s

DAVID BURNER
State University of New York at Stony Brook

ROBERT D. MARCUS
State University of New York at Stony Brook

THOMAS R. WEST
The Catholic University of America

HOLT, RINEHART AND WINSTON, INC.
New York   Chicago   San Francisco   Atlanta
Dallas   Montreal   Toronto   London   Sydney

Library of Congress Catalog Card Number: 70–155872

SBN: 03–085854–2

Printed in the United States of America

1 2 3 4   090   9 8 7 6 5 4 3 2 1

From Michigan, Indiana, and New York,
Bruce, Lorry, Guy, Roger, Sherry, Joe,
Cliff, Florence, Steve, Brunella,
Margaret, Bob, Mark, Tom, and others.

O, it is excellent
To have a giant's strength, but it is tyrannous
To use it like a giant!
     Measure for Measure, **II,** 2, 107–109

preface

Not so long ago "our times" meant two decades or more of an unbroken character. Now events quickly become distant and lost. The "March on Washington for Jobs and Freedom" of 1963, a climactic moment of the sixties, reflected a temper that we need almost a positive act of historical imagination to reconstruct. Time is no longer a broad band ringing our lives: it is a thin cruel edge. We feel our experience as past so soon, and our lives as history —a past with a pattern—scarcely at all.

To shape this inchoate past into formed history is not something that a few individuals can do. The historian writing of an earlier era has the advantage of all that students have done before him. The composing of history contemporary to the historian can be only a beginning to understanding—literally an essay, an attempt. The range of sources in a society devoted to its recordkeeping and prolific in its journalism is a treasure for succeeding generations; but it is a burden for the first historian who uses those sources. This is especially the case if he has absorbed the modern ethos of historical scholarship, which demands an account not only of doings among the mighty, but of the larger social forces and cultural trends. Yet a beginning must be made. If historians do not make that entry, other persons perhaps even less equipped with perspective or more in the grip of some prophetic urge will do so.

The authors of this history had their sensibilities formed in a more placid time than the one this book depicts, but our common awareness of the cultural and political limitations of the era in which we grew up has caused each of us in his own way to welcome the strenuous mind and emotion of the uncomfortable period through which we have lived. We have responded to it with both liking and mistrust and acknowledge that it has subtly molded us into different people. Committed to certain traditions, we have been forced into a deeper skepticism about them than we would have supposed. And even while we have been disillusioned with a liberalism of which the fruition in this decade was to be its passing, and have been drawn to the more imaginative politics of the sixties, we have in our own lives groped for a liberalism not yet articulated. The book is therefore a personal enterprise, as in some dimension history is always personal. It arose in part from our own need to make the decade pass into history, and we plan that as the sixties recede, our short preliminary essay toward understanding that time will grow with its authors into a fuller history. Meanwhile, we have met our own need to disenthrall ourselves —and we hope some of our readers.

Stony Brook, New York   D.B.
Washington, D.C.   R.D.M.
May 1971   T.R.W.

contents

ix

contents

A GIANT'S STRENGTH   America in the 1960s

a troubled affluence

Chapter One To a remarkable extent historians and popular
writers agreed on the mood of the 1950s: we had
entered upon a placid age, economically secure and
pleasantly dull. The affluent, even as they turned
from public issues to the suburban pursuit of
status, had surrendered their independence to corporations; Americans were absorbing from the
media a bland popular culture—"midcult," its
critics called it—that was neither vulgar nor serious
but simply insipid; they filled churches but made
the "American way of life" their religion; and they
raised children in amazing numbers. Commentators
noted an increasingly complicated structure of corporation, government, military, and academic bureaucracies in which procedures and methods were
more and more standard. America, they observed,
was flattening into a single unit as the West gained
population, the South industrialized, and indistin-

1

guishable suburbs sprang up from one end of the country to the other. Furthermore, as the critics rightly held, Americans were interested in making sure that their behavior was not in any way aberrant. The popularity of the Kinsey reports revealed how far this concern would go. Many people read them—or popularizations of them—avidly, hoping that their sexual life conformed to that of their neighbors.

While Americans were becoming uniform in certain matters, and a large part of the population (not so large as was then thought) had entered upon a remarkably comfortable economic existence, in other respects the American intellect was sharpening, the national conscience becoming more acute, and society was fracturing into new sorts of antagonistic interests and persuasions.

A major object of social and cultural criticism was standardization; and yet standardization held conflicting possibilities. The bleak surfaces of life could correspond, of course, to personalities bare of taste or imagination; and to the degree that they did so, all the talk about "conformity" had significance. Standardization could, however, mean something quite different. As people in increasing numbers moved to different sections of the country, from one suburb or urban development to another set of boxes in glass and brick, and abandoned everything that could sentimentally be called their "roots," they were forced to a flexibility and receptiveness of mind. Technology and the professions themselves demanded openness to new information and techniques. The major institutions set out to create a national and rootless class of managers and professionals; the corporations and the military moved their men about to teach them all phases of their work and to give them a national rather than a local orientation. Stripping away cluttered detail, cutting down the environment to its useful commodities and packaging those in neutral plastic, pulling families from neighborhoods and setting them in cubicles bare of personality, postwar technology could throw suburbanites and apartment dwellers back upon themselves and upon the advanced professional skills that gave them the place and identity their surroundings could not provide.

Standardization provided something more immediate. The repetitive institutions of the credit card, the chain store, and the quickly marketed fashions gave firmness of line to an unstable environment; the similar houses and shops and roads and name brands were little signposts for men and women unsure of their direction. Technology and rationalism cast a broad net over the land, but essential things slipped through.

Politically it was an unsettling age, not so much so as many others, but enough to dispel the myth of its blandness. Eisenhower prosperity was brief; the air of complacency that accompanied the installation of this beloved President was even more short-lived. The early fifties, the time of the Korean War and Joseph McCarthy, was a period of ideological and political stress. The breakdown of the wartime Russian-American alliance, the "fall" of China to the Communists, the Russian nuclear threat, the fear of internal subversion, and the emerging tensions over race marked by a split in the Democratic party—all had contributed to the irritable and sour malaise that Eisenhower's election was supposed to cure, and in fact did for a time. But the Eisenhower tranquillity did not last until the end of the General's administration. The political calm, which began only with the conclusion of the Korean War in mid-summer 1953, ended in October 1957 with the beeps from space of the Russian earth satellite. Criticisms of American politics grew all through the later fifties, and after the successful launching of a second vastly heavier Russian sputnik, the American public was quite ready to listen, as it demonstrated by electing a more liberal Congress in 1958.

Technology and economics put the continuing American phenomenon of migration, geographical and occupational, to a new point of activity in the fifties; communities were broken and others tentatively formed, and shifted populations congealed along dangerous fault lines—how dangerous would not be revealed for a number of years. The dominant continental motion was still westward; but now it was to the new Southwest as well, and into the old South, burgeoning with industries and cities. Of greater social consequence was the pattern of migration both in and out of the urban centers. Already in decay because depression and war had prevented the continual renovation they needed to remain habitable, the cities were undergoing a double movement that would damage them further. During the twenty-five years after 1930 there occurred an enormous movement off the farms and into the cities. By the 1950s twenty million people had flooded the cities; many impoverished rural blacks, country white southerners, Puerto Ricans, and Chicanos were victims of a technological revolution that enabled heavily mechanized farms to feed a nation approaching two hundred million. In the late forties and the fifties an even larger contrary shift was taking place, from the central cities to the peripheries; the urban middle classes, the modest and the affluent, were moving to the suburbs in search of better housing and schools. The passage to the suburbs was financed by wartime savings and postwar prosperity; it drew also on a gigantic federal subsidy to the middle classes in the form of mortgage guarantees, tax deductions, and road-building programs. These two migrations heightened the crisis of the city. The newcomers, poorly equipped culturally and economically for life in the continental metropolis, raised a demand for housing and public services inadequate to begin with, while families able to cope with big-city conditions and solvent enough to bear the tax burdens were leaving to enrich the school systems and the governments of the suburbs.

Suburbia was revealing some curious social patterns. Middle-class women were turning from the place in the world that their predecessors had gained throughout the century, and looking to their homes and kitchens, their car pools and their children. The proportion of women to the total college student population dropped steadily from 47 percent in 1920 to 35 percent in 1958; and the number of these women taking their degrees in secretarial, home economics, nursing, or teaching courses had risen to over half of the women enrolled. The proportion of women among professionals with Ph.D., LL.B., or M.D. degrees declined as well.

This trend admits of no simple explanation. American society has always exerted strong pressure to marry, and postwar prosperity removed inhibitions about wedding young. The median marrying age for women went down into the teens, and early marriages meant early childbearing. Add to this the responsibilities for uncompleted schooling, the isolation in bedroom suburbs where baby-sitting services are a perennial problem, and where time and transportation are major crises, and only special motivation would tempt a woman to combine her socially mandatory marriage with a career. The economy of the fifties, moreover, was not suited to her. Before the great university building boom got under way in the later fifties, there were too few professional schools even for the men who wished to attend them, and the G.I. Bill was, among many things, an act of *de facto* sexual discrimination applied to higher schooling. Women also suffered from the first misunderstandings of the postindustrial economy. Since muscle power was vanishing as a major asset, women were increasingly capable of performing the work the economy demanded; but the expansion of the consumer market was impressive. And the era was more conspicuous for the advertising bent on turning women into energetic consumers than for any attempts on the part of economists to discover job openings for them.

Suburban society was particularly child-centered. In the attenuated communities that extreme mobility produced, children were portable "roots" that peripatetic adults carried with them. The first social entree a new family might have into the neighborhood could occur when the mother heard of the local baby-sitting cooperative from other carriage-pushing women in the shopping center or the pediatrician's office. Churches grew enormously in membership, and their emphasis on family social services reflected the importance of the children. Suburbs were the milieu of adolescents. And adolescence—that long period of suspension before adulthood, in which the young are thrown together at school into their own society, given much leisure and much regimentation, equipped with records, radios, and cars, and learn that they are in a very particular and intriguing moment of their growing up—is a product of the twentieth century.

Early in the century most people scarcely had an adolescence by our social definition of it. They were children until they finished school (usually grade school), when they got a job and became adults. And child labor compelled some of them into man's or woman's estate even earlier. But in time an extensive adolescent subsociety took form, and by the late forties or earlier a number of its members had developed for themselves, and had received from fascinated adults, the self-image and style of hepcats and bobby-soxers.

It was a generation at school. Between 1900 and 1940 secondary education, once a small enterprise preparing a very few college-bound students and emphasizing grades and intellectual skills, became the nearly universal experience of youth in their teens. It had diluted its old curriculum with industrial and commercial courses, as well as with life-adjustment projects. These were intended to bring into the folkways of an urban industrial society the migrants from Europe and our own countryside, or their children. And then, after dropping for over forty years, the percentage of high school students going on to college began in the late forties to rise steeply, as America moved into a postindustrial economy demanding college graduates. Universities hastily expanded their facilities, first to meet the influx of returning veterans and then to accommodate the rush of students from the high schools and to prepare for the postwar babies. High schools and even primary schools returned to the function they had served before World War I, that of college preparation—but no longer for only a small segment of the people. The high schools, tied to an ideology of progressive education now under heavy intellectual attack and burdened with habits that had matured during the long era of practical, all-purpose secondary schools, strained to meet their new obligations. The attempt to raise standards, which went on through most of the decade but with increased intensity after the Russian space successes of 1957, pressed heavily upon the student population.

The affluent children of the fifties were not a gentry class assured of property and power whether they achieved academically or not, nor were they poor or lower-middle people who might believe that academic success would add increments to their future, a little more education meaning a little more wealth and standing. To the contrary, by the late fifties they were being taught to conceive of the world as an academic sweepstakes, where the very success not only of their own lives, but of their parents' as well, rested on their winning entry into the right college. The high school of the affluent was only the apex of an entire edifice built of educational playthings (not toys), nursery schools, "creative" summer camps, children's encyclopedias, and more homework. Parents invested energy in school budget fights and in parent-teacher associations. The new middle class was making of schooling, as the old had made of property, the ground of all progress; it was constituting itself a meritocracy. In the nineteenth century poverty and wealth had been defined by property, and the poor had been urged to work and save to acquire it; by mid-twentieth century poverty was understood to be qualitatively a lack of education, and one of the more interesting suggestions was to provide, as an incentive to parents and through them to their children, a payment to poor families for the achievements of their offspring at school.

The schools gave the adolescent society much of its character. The large high schools physically brought the young together; by the fifties, schools in affluent neighborhoods were virtually inclusive of youth, for the surrounding society did not siphon off many of the most admirable young people into adult roles as in the past, when school youths could see contemporaries already donning the mantle of the adult in the world of independence and financial reward. The relationships between the school and the student were differing and ambivalent. With the increasing professionalization of American society, college had become for middle-class youth a necessity, and if the teen-ager did not himself want to think a great deal about college, he had his parents to hover over his grades and ambitions, especially in the late fifties when competition for entrance into college became stiffer. The high school students who were taking their heroes not from the fields of intellectual and professional achievement but from athletics, modeling, and entertainment were nevertheless forced to base their future to some extent on performance in the classroom. Even the more intellectually relaxed of the schools required from the most relaxed students the persistent tedious business of attendance and at least exterior regimentation. James Coleman has described a passive resistance in which adolescent cliques imposed informal sanctions against excessive work and achievement on the part of their fellows. But in the dramatic rise in social importance that education was gaining during the later fifties some schools were becoming genuinely demanding and some students were getting a positive commitment to their work. For them the tensions of adolescence were increased by their anxieties of study.

Adolescent subsociety discovered and defined itself, though, not in its schooling but in its leisure—which, paradoxically enough, was enlarging in possibilities at a period when the pressures of education were also growing. Parents imposed less control. This was perhaps the first generation with sufficient money at its disposal that it could sustain a whole consumer market of its own. And an important part of that market was rock and roll.

Rock and roll is artistically important in its own light. Forms once distinctive, such as the jazz of the twenties and the swing of the thirties and after, had become by the forties and early fifties simply the common currency of American culture: the show tunes, the popular ballads, the "rhythm" numbers, all related distantly to their origins in Negro music but endlessly bleached by decades of adaptation. Song after song dealt in essentially the same tones, and was timed to fit one 10-inch 78 rpm record, published on the same street in Manhattan—dubbed Tin Pan Alley. Rock and roll was a fresh start. It got back to the rich lode of black music, added the sounds of country music, and devised new techniques for their transformation. The music and songs treated of special interests the young had found: the lovers, the hot rodders, the delinquents, the athletes, later the surfers, and especially the dancers and rockers themselves. Dick Clark's "American Bandstand," a popular television program that began in the summer of 1957, had a large impact; the program announced that the style had come into its own, persuaded young viewers that they could dare to dance in the new manner, and showed that performers need not be any older than they were. The hard beat of the music lent itself to an image and romantic myth that America was evolving about its youth: rock and roll seemed to express a young consciousness that was quick, syncopated, and at once tough and vulnerable. The music also evoked the technological setting, the advanced media and the fast cars, carefully and skillfully tended, for the sound had an almost metallic pace and brokenness.

This adolescent society was comparable only in a limited way to the more advanced youth culture of the sixties and beyond. It had no ideologies, no intentions to achieve permanence or to remake the rest of America; it was so much the object of commercialization that it seems almost to have been the passive recipient of its own self-image designed for it by its commercializers. Though doubtless it still exists, it has been overshadowed by the new culture of the universities and the streets, with their own styles now finding their way back into the high schools. But it did give something of itself to the more recent and more radical culture—beyond, of course, contributing those of its members who actually moved into that culture. It passed on its music, synthesized into folk rock and hard rock, and it hinted just barely at things that the counterculture explicitly believes in—a special consciousness, alien to the rest of civilization, new in perceptions, subsisting in its distinct community.

Beneath the surface of America in the fifties, the lives of black Americans were changing more than almost anyone realized. Their odyssey into the urban ghetto had its beginnings long ago; there had been heavy migration at the time of World War I, and even before. But the greatest influx started with the forties, when World War II cracked the old frozen customs of segregation. In 1940 the percentage of Negroes in occupations above the unskilled had actually been less than in 1890. But suddenly blacks were needed: the armed forces drew many of them, civilian employment opened as workers were pulled into the military services, and other jobs were created by the economic expansion of wartime. The eventual result of their exodus from the southern countryside to the cities would be the massive urban ghettos; but the war economy and the subsequent prosperity of the forties also gave birth to a new kind of middle class—more numerous and stronger than the older Negro bourgeoisie, more aggressive as it sensed its strength and had its initial provocative tastes of what equality might be like. And it was the first sizable segment of Negro society whose condition unequivocally committed it to the goal of integration.

The new urban, secularized Negro community produced a heady competition for power among a variety of organizations. The church was a declining, though continuing, social and political force in Negro life. Beside it the National Association for the Advancement of Colored People (NAACP) took leadership in the new bourgeoisie. With its continuous history of advocating legal, political, and social equality, the classic goals of integration, rather than the self-help of Booker T. Washington and the various Negro business groups, the NAACP spoke for the aspirations of the new black middle class, which was prepared to enter the white world with the aid of government and education instead of depending on business enterprise and community development. Moreover, the NAACP had achieved results. Its strategy of legal challenge to the edifice of segregation had earned victory after victory, starting with an important decision in 1938 to desegregate a law school and climaxing in *Brown* v. *Board of Education*, the famous school desegregation case of 1954.

As Negroes migrated northward they also shed their traditional allegiance to the party of Lincoln and became late arrivals in the New Deal coalition. Black Democratic Congressmen such as Oscar S. DePriest and William L. Dawson of Chicago, and Adam Clayton Powell of New York, gave witness that the movement out of the South had created a new political quantity. Under Presidents Roosevelt and Truman, Negroes received recognition in public office;

several important executive orders banned discrimination in industries related to war and integrated most of the armed forces. In 1948 the Democratic party leadership chose to accept a southern rebellion rather than alienate the liberal and black vote that it correctly diagnosed would provide the margin of victory in the populous northern states. Finally, in 1957, the first civil rights legislation in over eighty years passed through Congress. In that year as well, the crisis at Central High School in Little Rock, Arkansas, demonstrated that even a conservative administration would enforce Supreme Court rulings on the race question.

This political power, combined with the Court's decisions in favor of the Negro and the rise in economic position from the forties into the mid-fifties, brought forth a new temper in the black community, joining militancy about achieving rights to a considerable optimism over recent gains. The result was the remarkably good-natured and buoyant civil rights movement of the late fifties and early sixties, a movement whose main strength was the cooperation of liberal whites with the Negro middle class. Martin Luther King, Jr., emerged during the 1955 Montgomery, Alabama, bus boycott as the leading spokesman of the new mood. He translated legal advances into far wider social and moral energies. His tactics of direct action through nonviolent mass demonstration also made him the first black leader since Marcus Garvey in the 1920s to gain a large base of support in the community.

The fragility of this coalition should have been more obvious than it was. It rested not simply on the ability of white and black to cooperate politically; even more fundamentally it depended on the passive acquiescence of both black and white Americans outside the coalition. Almost certainly the majority of Americans never really approved of direct action as a technique. Northern whites would tolerate such activity only so long as they were not its targets. Any expansion of the civil rights movement beyond its assault on official segregation in the South might awaken their fears. And the passivity of lower-class Negroes lay on still more tenuous grounds. Until the early fifties, migration northward to better jobs had encouraged a sense of progress. But 1952 marked the point of closest parity to the white world, and the gap between white and black incomes began to increase once again. More and more blacks had grown up not in the South but in northern slums and had no memories of worse times by which to measure their progress; advertising and the new medium of television flaunted the affluence that other Americans enjoyed. The civil rights movement could sharpen this discontent, but not offer it an immediate practicable program. For much of the ghetto lived below the economic and social line at which integration is a possibility, unpossessed of skills and knowledge that would gain entrance to open employment, lacking the money to move into better neighborhoods, having access only to schools that would not be decent whether segregated or mixed. The new hopes raised in the fifties and the eroding life of the cities were uniting into a dangerous combination. By the end of the decade, white America discovered the Black Muslims, a small but suddenly growing nationalist sect vigorously opposed to integrating with "white devils." They were the "rainbow sign," as James Baldwin said: "No more water, the fire next time!"

America had a smaller band of rebels whose rebellion was singularly passive, expressing itself only through an engagement in an alternative way of life. Seeking poverty as a state of redemption, finding community among themselves, the "beats" proclaimed free perception and expressiveness—in cool jazz, in handicrafts or high arts, in drugs and sex, in exotic religion or poetry or mystic inspiration. Here were the ancient values of community and of the sensual, impulsive, and immediate life to pit against the abstraction, calculation, and hypocrisy of science, materialism, official religion, and the bureaucratic mind. Such a shrewd liberal publicist as James Wechsler instantly recognized the importance of the beats: although he was not happy with what Jack Kerouac and similar people were saying, he acknowledged them to be the first new voice to challenge his generation, which had come of age in the thirties. A purely personal and deliberately alienated movement like that of the beats could not provide the energies for rebellion, but their lives and their statement were a possible starting point for a more extensive cultural critique.

The citizens who came to be known as the "radical right" moved to the assertion of a separate identity. Those among them who had opposed the New Deal had known what it is to be among a frustrated minority; but for a period, the strident early days of the Cold War when "socialism" was a deadly word and hard-line Americanism was ascendant, the Right could assume that its temperament was the nation's. Many right-wingers have never abandoned that belief. But Dwight Eisenhower's triumph over the conservative Robert A. Taft in the 1952 Republican convention, the General's moderate administration, and the decline of McCarthyism, showed the Right that it no longer had a comfortable home in the Republican party and forced the more militant into a social and political enclave of their own. Particularly after the Cold War had become barren of the aggressive ideological emotion they relished, they formed secret groups like the John Birch Society and separate schools and institutions like the Christian Anti-Communist Crusade of Dr. Fred Schwartz, and published journals like *American Opinion*. In many areas they became active in local politics and on school and library boards, defending their neighborhoods from what they considered Communist penetration, and they maintained important pressures on American society. However far from their times these sour reactionary critics may have been, their fears of totalitarian centralism and their taste for smallness of scale were not unlike the persuasion that many on the Left would later have. The rightists were also suggestive of more recent movements in their coming to political awareness and their breaking away from a major party coalition; for it would be typical of the 1960s that social fragmentation would not remain social only, as it did for the most part in the Eisenhower years, but would find political expression.

The Cold War evoked a distinctive feeling for power: a sense of power in vast contours, the great antagonistic international blocs that were pressed against each other; a conception among informed Americans of the infinite detail, economic and technical, that sustains power; and for thoughtful segments of the public, a patient albeit nervous willingness to allow national policy the small exact moves, unsatisfying to chauvinism, that maintain power without inviting its violent eruption. To live with power so massive and ubiquitous, and learn so sophisticated an understanding of it, induced intellectual paradoxes that would become fully apparent only after about a decade of the Cold War. Civilization was thickening into great structures of technological power; yet in a few respects it was becoming light and spare. Technology itself worked increasingly with the invisible quickness of chemistry and electricity and nuclear fuel rather than with the bulky force of machines; the solid things of industrialism, the machinery and the buildings, continued their progress toward delicacy and perfection of line; and television was beginning to create a community of viewers that exists instantly and magically, in the obliteration of space.

Along with the technocratic rationalism of the Cold War went a careful, if not always successful, tempering of political tone. Even the Eisenhower administration, which was given at moments to describing international communism as a transcendent evil, was learning to speak in quieter tones. It was an age of making up material resources lost in depression and war, of muteness in criticism, and especially of horror over the excesses of political adventures. The memory of naziism traumatized a whole generation against activism and ideology in politics. Ideologies, both communist and fascist, were dangerous and irresponsible romantic visions, "terrible simplifications" that threatened civilized values. They were not only dangerous; they were unworkable, declared a doctrine proclaiming the "end of ideology": the world had become much too complex for simple solutions devised by theory and was now to be put in the hands of management, for piecemeal adjustment and sensible reform. This conception of politics, cool and rational, suited the problems of the Cold War, with its need for protracted and technically elaborate politics and for the avoidance of provocation and overreaction. In fact, the history of the idea was intimately tied to the Cold War. C. Wright Mills, one of its most powerful critics, observed that it "began in the mid-fifties, mainly in intellectual circles more or less associated with the Congress for Cultural Freedom and the magazine *Encounter*. . . . Since then, many cultural gossips have taken it up as a posture and an unexamined slogan." Actually it goes back to the very founding of the Congress for Cultural Freedom in 1950, and that organization, the *New York Times* discovered in April 1966, had been established and supported through its formative years by the United States Central Intelligence Agency. The Cold War had frozen some currents of intellectual life, drawing together government and the intellectual classes usually its critics. This went against a major tradition, for the conflict and tension between national claims and the life of the mind have persisted since the age of the French Revolution.

So unnatural an intellectual acquiescence could not continue. In Europe a recognizably newer Left emerged in both the eastern and NATO countries in a reaction to the events of 1956: the Suez crisis, the Russian invasion of Hungary, and Khrushchev's revelations (at the twentieth party congress) of Stalin's crimes. The whole system of international power politics that was the common creation of the two great foes would soon face major attacks. By the end of the decade, a Marxist radicalism was spreading to a few American campuses. Wisconsin had an active socialist club that began publishing *Studies on the Left* in 1959, the first important journal of the evolving new Left. At Berkeley in that year SLATE was organized to run independent candidates for student government. Graduate students at the University of Chicago began publishing *New University Thought* in 1960. Minor episodes of campus activism occurred.

Further questionings came from professional critics. While the social sciences were in many cases deeply involved with the government in its decision making, and organizations like the Rand Corporation did direct consulting for policy makers, social science was also a ground of social criticism. In fact, the role that journalists had performed earlier in the century, that of "muckraking" the nation to uncover the evils buried beneath the official pieties, was now frequently performed by social scientists. Economists analyzed the poor performance of the American economy in the light of European and Japanese growth rates. Sociologists raised the specter of conformity and the "organization man." They also analyzed and decried status seeking and subliminal advertising. John Kenneth Galbraith exposed poverty and the decline of public services in the midst of affluence. C. Wright Mills described America as a mass society ruled by an interlocking power elite. Mills, the most radical of the sociological muckrakers, aptly described the function he served: "When little is known, or only trivial items publicized, or when myths prevail, then plain description becomes a radical fact, or at least is taken to be radically upsetting." This new sociological muckraking found its popularizers in journalism, and such writers as Vance Packard came to make the social sciences their journalistic beat, presenting the findings of social investigators without the charts, graphs, and qualifications. Late in the decade, after the Russian space achievements, liberal Americans increasingly became willing to listen to the various kinds of criticism; many of the Kennedy programs were a result. Dwight Eisenhower himself, a man of the era that was passing, warned about the existence of a "military-industrial complex" and thereby contributed a phrase that before long would be popular on the Left.

The loosening of debate went back to a number of tangible developments in domestic and international affairs. America's age of renewed social criticism was part of the "thaw" that appeared to envelop the entire world in the late fifties. The postwar era, moreover, the period defined by the problems World War II had created, was coming to an end. The economic and social troubles of the world were increasingly those of the new nations, the new economies, and a new generation growing up since the war. And the lessons of the past, always infinitely malleable, would change as well. Even the central lesson of modern history, the possibility of a regime such as the Nazis', altered its meaning. Watching the trial of Adolf Eichmann in Jerusalem in 1961, the world saw a new side to the horrors of totalitarianism: that it was, as Hannah Arendt explained, the product not only of mad romantic demagogues, but of the rational, pragmatic, sensible bureaucrats who ran the machinery of the state—or, indifferently, the machinery of death. We might avoid madmen with luck, but how were we to escape from the technocrats whom every modern society seemed to need and whose reasoned attitudes we had trusted to save us from the romantic, the irresponsible, and the sinister?

Freshmen at Southern Illinois University, 1960. (Francis Miller, LIFE Magazine © Time Inc.)

Dick Clark, American Bandstand Show, 1959. (UPI)

Suburban housing, 1960s. (Charles Gatewood)

Allen Ginsberg reading poetry in Washington Square Park. (Charles Gatewood)

A beatnik, 1950s. (Laurence Fink)

Kennedy-Nixon televised debates. Election year 1960. (Pictorial Parade)

Fidel Castro and Nikita Khrushchev at opening session of the United Nations General Assembly, 1960. (Wide World)

President Kennedy and former President Eisenhower at Camp David, 1961. (Wide World)

Alan Shepard, America's first spaceman, is lifted into a helicopter after his suborbital flight from Cape Canaveral (now Cape Kennedy), Florida, 1961. (Wide World)

Cutaway version of survival shelter, 1960. (Nassau County Civil Defense Office)

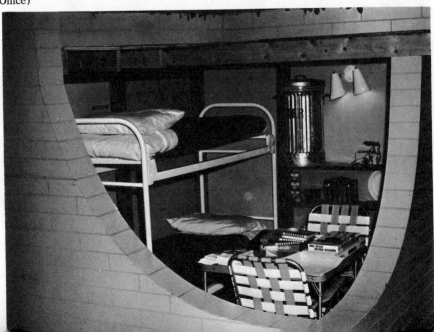

The Military Industrial Complex

NEWSWEEK magazine cover. (Drawing by Flora)

Soviet-developed Cuban missile base, 1962. (UPI)

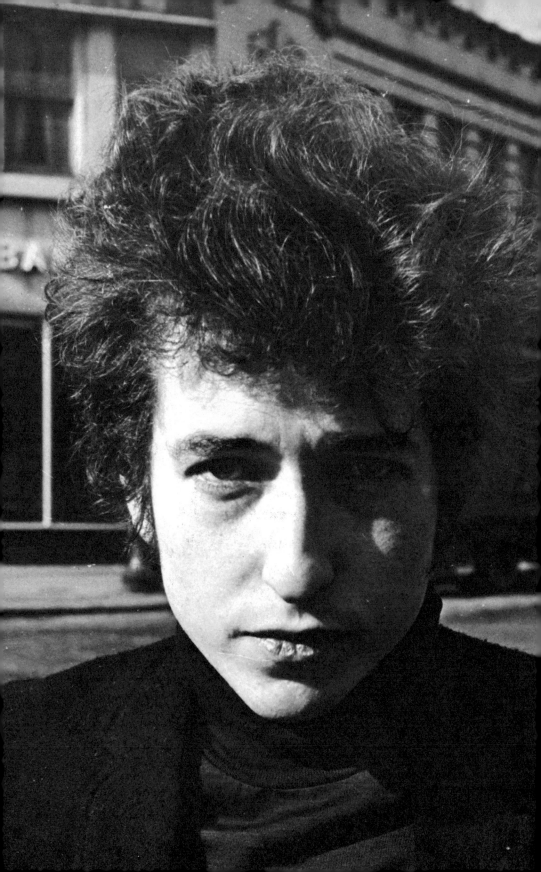

Bob Dylan, 1965. (Fred McDarrah)

Peace Corps volunteer teaching English to Philippine Islanders. (UPI)

First Buddhist monk to protest the government in South Vietnam by self-immolation, 1963. (Wide World)

(Wide World)

President John F. Kennedy. (Elliott Erwitt, Magnum)

Jack Ruby aiming revolver at Lee Harvey Oswald, accused assassin of President Kennedy. (Wide World)

After the swearing-in, President and Mrs. Johnson try to comfort Mrs. Kennedy. (UPI)

The funeral of John F. Kennedy, November 1963. (Ken Heyman)

(Ken Heyman)

Art Reproductions. 3 for $1.00. (Ken Heyman)

kennedy: a cold warrior

Chapter Two   John F. Kennedy came to the office of President as a spokesman for the Cold War at its most sophisticated point. The nation had acquired, during a decade of atomic diplomacy, an intelligence and temperament that enabled it to live with some coolness amidst the continuing strategies and extraordinary technological complex of nuclear confrontation. The language of that intelligence was Kennedy's: he could speak crisply about the dangers of a missile gap, the need for innovation in nuclear weaponry, the advantages of flexible response over massive retaliation. He combined a fascination for military technology with a feeling for military dash and elitism; a naval hero who had survived a bizarre shipwreck, a reader of James Bond novels, he was intrigued by the knowledge that we had it within our ability to fly a specially trained army from New Jersey to Asia in two days, and he admired the Green Berets, telling them to wear their insignia proudly.

31

The flaws in the temperament of the Cold War strategists are easy to define. In our recent rediscovery of high political emotion, we have learned to condemn past administrations for bringing to desperately human facts little more than the calculations of a computerized intelligence. But that temperament had its special strengths of nerve and patience; and in its quickness to perceive complications, its analytical dislike of ideological formulas, it carried the seeds of its own liquidation. Kennedy was both in person and in time a figure central to that paradox; the Cold War as an assured attitude of mind would not long survive his presidency. Like other technicians of the conflict, from George F. Kennan and Dean Acheson onwards, the President did not want to talk the anti-Communist ideology of the Right —that would be too simplistic and would distract us from the details of power and the diversities in local situation with which our strategies had to cope. Yet if we were to forbear obsessions about the existence of a monolithic international communism and instead think of peasant revolutions and emergent nationalism and tension among Communist states, then we were obliged to prepare for a time when the world quasi war would no longer be necessary, and at that instant to effect quick disengagements. But Kennedy would not himself live to preside over a policy finally twisted and broken with self-contradiction, as it pursues in Vietnam a conflict that its own habit of careful calculation puts into question; and a conflict for which it cannot allow itself a satisfyingly belligerent and chauvinistic rhetoric, for it does not believe in such rhetoric.

Kennedy's unconscious part in all this was to an extent a matter of his sophistication in rhetoric, his insistence during the 1960 campaign, for example, that the developing split between China and Russia should dominate our view of communism. After Kennedy, critics could no longer condemn the mentality of the Cold War for its simplicity; they would need to rebut the complex and highly qualified understanding it had reached. Kennedy had something else to do with the psychology of the decade. He contributed to the youth movement that by the later sixties succeeded in making a major statement against the structures of American power. His appeals to idealism and to sacrifice struck a responsive chord, and beyond these intangibles his administration attracted young people into lives of public service. Kennedy also gave cover and encouragement to the civil rights workers in the South, the early activists of liberation and communalism. Yet even in all this the bite of mind that he brought to nuclear diplomacy was also the verve of his domestic politics. The call to arms was cool and tempered: Kennedy once told a group of White House reporters that he had little faith anything he could do would solve America's problems. He seemed to believe in human depravity.

Though many of John Kennedy's beliefs grew out of the 1950s, his personal manner had set him far apart from other politicians of that decade: he disdained the cronyism of the Senate, the cant of national politicians, and the naiveté of the professional liberals. Toward such things he showed an aristocrat's aloofness, even an arrogance born of having money, brains, good looks, the right education, a war hero's record, a beautiful wife, and a father ambitious for his son. Kennedy's temperament, detached from some accepted values and without illusions, was quite compatible with a manipulation of the electorate. When he first entered presidential politics in 1956 as a candidate for the vice-presidency, he let his adviser Ted Sorenson circulate a memorandum arguing that a Catholic candidate would strengthen rather than harm a national ticket. In 1959 he told a group of Pennsylvanians that if he went into the convention with many delegates and then were denied the nomination, the Democratic party would risk alienating Catholics and losing the election. Such incidents foreshadowed the opportunistic way Kennedy would use his Catholicism in the 1960 campaign, and they created a lasting impression of Kennedy as a man in a hurry.

Kennedy's coolness of manner protected his integrity. Never possessed of a political street personality, he winced at the thought of displaying his emotions. His critical mistake at the 1956 Democratic Convention, where he sought the vice-presidency, was in not visiting Hubert Humphrey to win favor—or so one account has it. The chosen candidate, Estes Kefauver, indulged in a tearful meeting with the sentimental Humphrey that would have been foreign to Kennedy's temper. Senator Kennedy, who had lost potential votes by declaring against high price supports for farmers, barely missed the vice-presidential nomination in 1956, and perhaps he did not try very hard. But it was a lucky thing: a place on the losing ticket would have spoiled his perfect record at the polls, and he was free to win a record-breaking reelection victory from Massachusetts voters in 1958.

Kennedy's record in the House and Senate had been marred by his failure to speak out against the demagogic Senator Joseph McCarthy —a failure especially to be noted in the author of *Profiles in Courage;* he missed the important censure vote because of sickness and did not arrange to pair with some member opposed to censure. He did not lead in introducing new legislation. Yet he was an independent man, usually given to an honest expression of his political views. He supported the St. Lawrence Seaway, despite its unpopularity in

Massachusetts; though a decorated veteran, he condemned the powerful American Legion on the floor of the House; an Irishman, he was
the only Democratic congressman in his state not to request a pardon
for James Michael Curley, the former governor and congressman
popular among the Irish in Massachusetts and then serving a term in
prison. Kennedy had about him an air of freshness and unpredict-
ability. He was both Irish and a Harvard graduate; he was wealthy,
yet was presumed a political underdog because of his religion. His
coolness of manner even hinted at a new type of popular hero.

The success of Senator Kennedy and other congressional Democrats
in the elections of 1958—a crucial moment in the realignment of
forces that was to change the politics of the era—gave political
expression to an awareness of things wrong with American society.
Older conservatives such as Senators William Knowland, John
Bricker, and William Jenner disappeared from national life, and
many of the new faces of the sixties first appeared in the Congress
that met the following year. The Russian space achievement in sending two sputniks across the sky in 1957 had particularly shocked the
country. American scientific education became a major campaign
issue for Democrats, and was intensified by the crowding of the
enormous postwar generation into inadequate school facilities across
the nation. Publicists pointed to still more failures in American
society: the coexistence of poverty and affluence; alleged corporate
control over American foreign policy; uninhabitable suburbs under-
supplied with libraries, parks, and privacy; and a conformity that
threatened boredom and demoralization among the very class of
technicians and businessmen who might have supplied America with
new initiatives. While not all of these were politically effective issues,
they contributed to a growing unease.

Most of all, the sluggish economy injured Republican candidates.
The Eisenhower administration had discovered the means to prevent
depression, but it seemed powerless to avoid repeated recessions, to
stem inflation, or even to achieve a national economic growth rate
at levels then prevailing in Western Europe or the Soviet Union. That
failure came at a bad time. For a rise in productivity for each man-
hour created surplus labor that demanded an economy expansive
enough to supply it with jobs, while accumulating social needs and
programs in health, welfare, and education required a richer economy
yielding tax receipts adequate to finance them.

Though Democrats, including Senator Kennedy, blamed the inaction on Treasury Secretary George Humphrey's strong influence with
Eisenhower, the cause cut deeper, for the peculiar way the economy
had solved some of its older problems had generated new ones.
Trusts had settled down into a permanent state to which economists

gave the ugly name "oligopoly"; large firms were attempting to run their sectors of the economy not for the venturesome efforts of competition but for the comforts of profits at high prices. Much of the labor problem had been solved by wage increases to a unionized elite of protected workers, often in the same enterprises that were also organized into oligopoly. Gains in wages for the protected workers were passed on to consumers in the form of a general rise in prices. The situation of the unemployed meanwhile remained static because surplus capital was being consumed in the form of inflation long before it turned to new production and new jobs. Investments in plants and equipment shrank; late in the decade investments in the United States for these crucial items were one-eighth those of European countries in proportion to population.

The Eisenhower administration was too firmly grounded in the business community to press for serious changes in economic policy. Undoubtedly, it sincerely desired to stem price increases, but it could make no move at all when business, particularly the steel industry, resisted. The conditions of the late 1950s pose curious questions about the history of fiscal and economic policy. It is a standard assumption that the forces of business and the political Right have tended to favor economic opportunity over social justice. Yet the 1950s present the spectacle of a business-dominated government that seems to have restrained economic growth, while the liberal forces of the late fifties and the early sixties made growth their major domestic objective. Although such influences as simple hostility to the new economics also shaped its thinking, the business community —and its allies in the Republican party—took far longer than most economists, politicians, and publicists to recover from the trauma of the Great Depression.

While unemployment rates went as high as 7.5 percent, their political impact on organized labor, an elite working in heavy industry and participating in Eisenhower prosperity, was remarkably small. But conservative business groups politicized labor in the 1958 elections by placing the open or nonunion shop ("right to work" law) on the ballot in several states. And nonorganized workers were not going to continue being thankful for the absence of outright depression when a sharp recession in 1957–1958 was followed by a weak recovery of only twenty-five months, retarded afresh by a lengthy steel strike, and that in turn coasting into new recession in 1960–1961.

Disadvantaged groups in America suffered most from these economic slackenings. Negroes were flooding into urban ghettos, Indians and Mexicans were lost in self-perpetuating poverty, and growing numbers of elderly men and women were living out useless lives in decaying rooms or becoming medical indigents in hospitals that lacked not simply adequate medical care but often rudimentary cleanliness. Such people, as Michael Harrington pointed out in an unforgettable term, were "invisible" in the 1950s. In part this meant that they were physically shut away: in hospitals, on reservations, in migrant workers' camps, on the other side of freeways, or in inner cities abandoned by the middle class. But they were also politically invisible, without organized groups among themselves or representation through any other group, such as the Democratic party fixed to its institutional base in the unions. The fifties lacked an intellectual as well as a workers' Left; and this means not so much that the country was deprived of the specific policies such a Left might have achieved but that the conservative administration was able to be much more conservative, having no articulate opponent able to compel concessions from it.

John Kennedy knew his times well and believed he could cope with their problems. His near success in winning the vice-presidential nomination in 1956, and his enormous victory in the 1958 Massachusetts Senate race, made him a serious candidate for the presidency in 1960. The absence of other strong Democratic candidates was another advantage for Kennedy. Some party professionals thought he alone might pull back into the Democratic party the many Catholic voters who had deserted it in 1952 and 1956. Nevertheless, the party's leaders worried about his religion and his youthfulness. Since Al Smith's crushing defeat in 1928 still haunted the party, Kennedy would first have to show in the primaries that he could attract solid support from Protestants. His unimpressive victory over Hubert Humphrey in the early Wisconsin primary did not prove the point, for that state had too many Catholic voters. West Virginia, where he was scheduled to contest the persistent Humphrey on May 10, would be the crucial field of the preconvention campaign.

Kennedy's advisers told him to play down the religious issue in West Virginia. But average West Virginians, Kennedy instinctively believed, knew they were being tested and that their vote, above all else, would be interpreted by the nation at large as a repudiation or an endorsement of bigotry. Humphrey vehemently attacked the candidate's wealth, but West Virginians, like other Americans, admire wealth; and besides, Kennedy appeared moved by what he saw of poverty in the state. Kennedy himself repeatedly drew attention to his religion; he used the issue in a way that his opponent could not, managing to make it a matter of sportsmanship. West Virginia, a state 95 percent Protestant and only 4 percent black, cast 61 percent of its Democratic primary vote for Kennedy.

The victory in West Virginia carried Kennedy to a first-ballot nomination in Los Angeles. The Democratic Convention in that city was graced by Senator Eugene McCarthy's eloquent plea for the nomination of Adlai E. Stevenson, twice defeated as the party's presidential candidate: "Do not reject this man who made us all proud to be called Democrats. . . ." But Stevenson's candidacy, which he suspected was engineered by the Johnson people in an effort to head off the main contender, irritated Kennedy. When a close election seemed in the offing, why did Stevenson let liberals rally in an impossible drive against the front-runner? For him and for Eleanor Roosevelt the reason was to keep Kennedy aware that his record needed to be more daring. But the Senator believed Stevenson's bid to be a hopeless and egotistical gesture certain to endanger party unity, and the venture by the Stevenson forces did not stop Kennedy from offering the vice-presidency to a man unpopular among northern liberals—Lyndon Baines Johnson.

Much has been written about the selection of Johnson, who had held second place in the presidential balloting. Most of the accounts treat the offer and the acceptance as spontaneous and even impulsive; this may be true but both men, who respected each other considerably, must also have been calculating the likelihood for months: such a ticket would certainly be the strongest one imaginable. The Republican candidate, Richard Nixon, knowing this, had anticipated the ticket. The least measurable issue of the campaign, Kennedy's religion, presented the worst handicap in the South, where the Texas Protestant Johnson would greatly aid the ticket. Johnson was well regarded among farmers, businessmen, and conservative independents in the rest of the country, many of whom might have been expected to lean toward Nixon. Such voters would be attracted by Johnson's prudent legislative record, his willingness to cooperate with Eisenhower, and his universally acknowledged political skill at leading the Democratic party in the Senate. True, Johnson's candidacy would not be good news to labor and the liberals—but where else could they go? Nixon, they had decided long ago, was beyond redemption. Apparently the vice-presidency also suited the ambitions of Johnson, who had offered to run with Stevenson in 1956; the office would lift him above a confining Southern identity, which had stood in the way of the presidential nomination.

Johnson went on to conduct a superbly professional campaign. Kennedy, in Norman Mailer's image, was a young professor whose manner was adequate for the classroom, but whose mind was off in some intricacy of the Ph.D. thesis he was writing; the man was always a touch too aloof from the candidate. Johnson, on the other hand, gave all of himself: he was "a political animal, he breathed like an animal, sweated like one, you knew his mind was entirely absorbed with the compendium of political fact and maneuver." On his brilliant campaign trips through the South, Johnson demanded order and precision: the rostrum had to be exactly 52 inches high when he spoke, the band must blast the first note of "The Yellow Rose of Texas" the second he finished speaking, the train must pull away from the station at the syllable of farewell. The content of Johnson's message as he sped from one small town to another— "God bless yuh, Rocky Bottom. Ah wish ah could stay an' do a little sippin' an' whittlin' with yuh. . . . God bless yuh, Gaffney"—seemed to clash oddly with the technical skill of the performance and the abrupt manners of the candidate among his advisers but apparently spoke to his audience.

Kennedy's Republican opponent, Vice-President Nixon, was a strong candidate. Much more attuned to the country's politics than Dwight Eisenhower, he had been an active and partisan Vice-President, urging his administration to take a more progressive view on civil rights, the economy, and public education. He was effective on television and welcomed the chance to debate Kennedy. Newspaper editors and publishers generally favored Nixon, and his campaign chest more than matched Kennedy's. His greatest fault was one that John Kennedy spotted easily: Nixon lacked taste. He fabricated sentimentality and sought a level of communication much below his capacity.

Nixon's campaign was fated to a series of misfortunes. His running mate, Henry Cabot Lodge, proved to be an unenthusiastic campaigner. A preconvention meeting at Governor Nelson Rockefeller's New York apartment was interpreted by many Republican conservatives as a capitulation to Rocky's liberal domestic views. Early in the campaign, Nixon suffered an infected knee and was hospitalized for two weeks; later, still underweight and in a weakened condition, he caught a bad case of the flu. Despite the loss in time, he insisted on fulfilling a pledge to visit all fifty states, spending valuable hours in Alaska when he should have been barnstorming downstate Illinois. Instead of benefiting from Eisenhower's projected meeting with Khrushchev at Paris in the spring of 1960, Nixon shared with the administration the embarrassment of being caught in the act of espionage; a short time before, an American U-2 high-altitude reconnaissance plane had been shot down deep in Russian territory. Thereby the Republican slogan of peace and prosperity, already in doubt because of the continuing recession, suffered a further loss of credibility. In August, Eisenhower was none too helpful when he carelessly told a reporter who had asked him what major administration decisions Nixon had participated in: "If you give me a week, I might think of one." And Nixon could not make good use of Eisenhower in the closing weeks of the campaign, for the President's doctors advised against it. When the Reverend Norman Vincent Peale, Nixon's New York pastor, condemned Kennedy on religious grounds, the minister in fact lent strength to the argument that a vote for a Catholic was a vote for freeing politics of the sterile religious issue. The incident gave Kennedy an opportunity dramatically to convince an audience of Houston ministers that they had no call to fear him. Worst of all, a series of television debates demolished the myth of Kennedy's youthful inexperience and placed the haggard Nixon in the role of defending a passive administration. The Vice-President had counted on his ability: there was the effective "kitchen debate" of 1959 with Khrushchev in Moscow; and in a television speech of the 1952 campaign, when Nixon defended himself against dubious allegations of financial misconduct and evoked the name of his dog, Checkers, he had proved his mastery of television. He could not strike hard, since he thought it unwise to evoke memories of his ruthlessness in anti-Communist investigation during the McCarthy era, and in any case Kennedy kept him off balance.

Once Eisenhower had set the depression psychosis to rest, the nation was ready to venture beyond tranquillity to a more exciting economics of expansion, and this the young Kennedy offered it. Economic experiment came to seem not only possible but necessary if America was to maintain a position of world leadership. The Cold War, which for so long had hampered experimentation, now encouraged it, for Russia was embarked on a phase of economic competition with the United States. Khrushchev's threat "We will bury you," by which he signified economic triumph, illustrates that the Cold War was shifting from direct confrontation to a struggle for the Third World, whose need for development meant that the United States and Russia had to compete as models of productivity. Kennedy, by shrewdly emphasizing a missile gap and Castro's victory in Cuba, and by linking the issues of national prestige and economic growth, implied that Nixon—part of a well-intentioned but ineffective administration—could not solve these difficulties. The two party platforms, an aggressive Democratic document and a defensive Republican one, seemed to restate the difference between the candidates.

During the campaign Kennedy rarely attacked the substance of the Eisenhower foreign policies. But citing a supposed missile gap, he urged that we catch up with Russia technologically, particularly in space. With problems like Cuba and Laos in mind, Kennedy also called for a new look for the army. A one-sided reliance on nuclear weapons—the "bigger bang for the buck" philosophy of Eisenhower's Defense Secretary Charles E. Wilson—denied us any flexibility of choice, Kennedy argued. Faced with a war of national liberation, we were restricted to the alternatives of doing nothing or threatening a nuclear strike, and that threat could not be carried out except at a catastrophic price. Perhaps, of course, Eisenhower and Dulles never really thought nuclear war to be an option. Conceivably they believed that no aggressive military move by Russia was likely and that our opposition to localized revolts would have to take nonmilitary form. Eisenhower himself talked of peace and offered his "open skies" disarmament proposal; his own enormous prestige enabled him stubbornly to resist enlarged military appropriations and to criticize influential generals and admirals as "parochial." Kennedy, on the other hand, proposed that the nation complement its nuclear arsenal with a well-financed, innovative armed force and an improved stock of conventional weapons. He was capitalizing on a debate in the Pentagon itself; for such army leaders as Maxwell Taylor and Matthew Ridgway were calling for a more mobile and sophisticated force capable of fighting in limited kinds of unrest such as that in Laos and the Congo. Kennedy's kinetic charm (he talked too fast for most people to grasp his arguments) and his confidence in fathoming the complexity of public problems cast him as a man with a more sophisticated, more dashing, and more effective response to the familiar problems of the fifties. He defeated Nixon by 303 to 219 electoral votes and by a hairsbreadth in the popular vote. Even the electoral vote in truth should have been closer: alleged fraud in counting the close returns in Illinois and Texas cast deep suspicion on the Kennedy victory in those states. Any Democrat should have won easily given the recession and the strength of his party. It is puzzling that Kennedy did not do better. Whether his religion helped or harmed him is questionable. The Survey Research Center of the University of Michigan, and other similar organizations, found that the issue cost him 2 percent of the popular vote but helped him in crucial states with substantial Catholic blocs and large electoral votes.

In the course of his presidency, Kennedy would eventually articulate a foreign policy of restraint and accommodation, and bring the Cold War almost to the point of its terminating in explicit agreements and implicit understandings. Yet he came to the office with a remarkable bellicosity. John Kennedy, Congressman and Senator from 1947 to 1960, was a product and, like almost everyone of that era, a prisoner to some extent of the Cold War. He had matured from its earlier rhetoric—he apologized for blaming the loss of China on the Truman administration—he had profited from its growing sophistication, and he hoped, with Eisenhower, for an eventual accommodation with Russia. But he was of two minds, for he also appeared to believe that communism would continue to be America's

implacable foe. In Kennedy's years in the House of Representati
that body had habitually voted overwhelmingly for resolutions c
ing on the peoples of eastern Europe to revolt against their Communist rulers; and Kennedy had joined in these votes. Anticommunism,
moreover, was a strong tradition of Kennedy's own family and
church. In the first television debate with Nixon he endorsed a devil
theory of communism.

President Kennedy's selection of advisers like Dean Rusk for State,
Robert McNamara for Defense, and Walt Rostow and McGeorge
Bundy as White House aides showed he was not ready for a foreign
policy like that of Adlai Stevenson, who had been almost alone in
believing, as early as 1956, that the Cold War might conceivably be
liquidated. Kennedy chose his staff from organization men who
held positions demanding great technical competence in government, business, or university bureaucracies. He finally rejected independent figures like Senator William Fulbright, his own initial
favorite for the post of State. Rusk, who became a strong, and stubborn, Secretary of State, failed at first to provide leadership. Mc-
Namara, a man of some genius, talked of "cost-effectiveness" and
"flexible response," but rarely if ever disagreed with a unanimous
decision of the Joint Chiefs of Staff. Hawkish former Secretary of
State Dean Acheson gave his approval to the Kennedy appointments,
recommending Rusk after warning that the selection of Stevenson
for State would be a "terrible disaster" and that of Fulbright a "mistake." If the year 1960 had a tone in foreign policy, it was set by the
publication of Herman Kahn's *On Thermonuclear War*, which Kennedy studied closely. Kahn, who thought war likely and described
how we could survive, argued that if Russia braced for a nuclear
attack and America did not, our world position would be weakened.

The beliefs on foreign policy that Kennedy carried with him into
office are caught for history in the Bay of Pigs fiasco. The Eisenhower
administration, to be sure, had prepared the way for anti-Communist
guerrillas to invade Cuba. More than a thousand Cuban refugees,
trained by America's Central Intelligence Agency, awaited commands
at a coffee plantation high in the Guatemalan mountains. To cancel
the planned invasion and disperse the men, who would tell tales,
might say to the world that the new administration in Washington
was weak. To some degree, events generated their own momentum,
and Kennedy received misinformation and bad advice from the CIA.
He had also seen that the increasingly dictatorial Castro had deceived
many liberals, and he had his own jingoistic campaign rhetoric to
live with. Finally, the bureaucracies of government, during the Bay
of Pigs and later in the Vietnam escalations, discouraged criticism
and "rocking the boat"; here Kennedy might have been saved by the

visceral liberals his temperament could not abide. Still, it was absurd to suppose that the well-entrenched Castro could be overthrown without the active support of the United States Air Force, Army, and Navy; and to make an abortive attempt would be disastrous. Cuba, as Senator Fulbright observed, was after all a thorn in the flesh, not a dagger in the heart. The important creditable part of the President's role came in restraining the militarists who wanted an all-out attack when it was plain that the landing had failed.

How could a hardheaded pragmatist like Kennedy have been misled by advisers he hardly even knew? It was perhaps a part of his competitive temper that drove him almost to court crisis; in the inaugural, for instance, he had declaimed, "Before my term has ended we shall have to test anew whether a nation organized and governed such as ours can endure." He repeatedly declared America to be at the most critical point in its history. In those days he even gave serious thought to a planned assassination of Castro, according to a source perhaps inaccurate, Senator George Smathers. In 1962 he told the journalist Stewart Alsop that a nuclear war in the next decade stood an even chance. Some part of the decision to place our prestige on the line with the guerrilla invaders, however, must also have been based on the faulty premise that because communism was totalitarian the people who lived under it yearned for freedom and would revolt at the first opportunity. And since communism was evil, the rebels would succeed. They failed miserably. Their CIA-directed strategy included every blunder imaginable: the wrong landing place, inadequate air cover, munitions and equipment piled in a single boat, and an underestimation of the enemy's strength.

In the short term, the Bay of Pigs possibly taught Kennedy the wrong lesson: it firmed his resolve to expect and be prepared for future encounters, and he redoubled his efforts to increase military spending. Though he also pushed the Alliance for Progress, seeking to reconstruct Latin America economically, he discounted arguments that building up an arsenal of conventional weapons would itself be a provocative act demanding a like response from the Soviets.

The first years of the Kennedy administration were a brief but dangerous period in international relations. During these times the old policy of threatening a massive nuclear retaliation existed perilously alongside a new problem, the national liberation movements. In Asia, in Africa, and in Latin America, in countries like Laos, the Congo, and Cuba, dynamic revolutionary forces were challenging the world balance of power. In the fresh context of the sixties, irresponsible third powers might precipitate the ultimate conflict between Russia and the United States.

In the long, tense confrontation over Berlin that lasted throughout

1961, Kennedy seemed to believe that an actual war could break out, that Russian determination might force war. Such was his impression from talking with Khrushchev at the summit meeting held in Vienna in June 1961; the Russian leader said that before the end of the year his country would sign a treaty with East Germany banning us from West Berlin. The encounter deeply troubled Kennedy, and shortly afterward he spurred fallout shelter construction, increased draft quotas, and called up military reserve units. For some years Russia had appeared to be ahead in space, in industrial growth, in long-range missiles; and it seemed that Communist imperialism was making progress almost everywhere in the world except Western Europe, where, since NATO and the Marshall Plan, communism had stopped its advance. At Vienna Khrushchev sharply challenged Kennedy even in Europe, demanding that the West sign a German peace treaty or quit Berlin. Stiffened by the hard-line opinion of Dean Acheson that Berlin was a "simple conflict of wills," Kennedy saw Khrushchev's "ultimatum" as an audacious effort to upset the one area of the world where America was incontestably ahead.

Khrushchev eventually compromised on Western Europe, constructing the Berlin wall and withdrawing the deadline of January 1, 1962, for Western acquiescence. In the long run, the wall was a propaganda triumph for the West. But international tension continued to tighten in 1962. The previous summer and fall Kennedy had sped his plan for building fallout shelters. America's increased defense spending provoked a comparable rise in Russia. In response to Khrushchev's resumption of atmospheric nuclear testing in the fall of 1961, Kennedy followed suit the next April. In Africa, Russia and Communist China slipped from the toehold they had gained around the turn of the decade. The United Nations was instrumental in preserving the new Congo nation and in blocking a Soviet-American clash there; and Kennedy scored a coup by an order denying arms to South Africa as long as it should practice hard racial separation. On the other hand, although Khrushchev managed to effect a neutralization of Laos, indigenous Communist movements were gaining ground in South Vietnam, Cambodia, and the Philippines. In reaction, Kennedy, appealing to American pride, competitiveness, anticommunism, and respect for technology, secured enormous congressional appropriations for military purposes and for the race to the moon, which the President promised to reach before the end of the decade.

Then in the autumn of 1962 the world came as close as it ever has come to destruction. During the preceding summer Khrushchev had decided to place long-range nuclear missiles in Cuba. Once again, the Central Intelligence Agency failed Kennedy on Cuba; Senator Kenneth Keating of New York, using Cuban refugees as his source, seemed to be able to guess more about the missiles than the administration. Not until mid-October was it known definitely in Washington that Russian missiles in Cuba were aimed at principal American cities. The immediate reaction was one of astonishment. Nowhere else in the world outside its own borders had Russia set up such missiles. The tactical advantage was slight; Russian submarines equipped with similar weapons had been passing close to American shores for many years. But from a diplomatic standpoint the interference in an area so patently within America's sphere of influence was flagrant.

At first Kennedy's advisers considered every alternative course of action, but soon two groups coalesced, one advising an air strike and the other some kind of blockade. The Joint Chiefs favored the more warlike course, even though it would probably kill Soviet technicians. Robert Kennedy persuasively argued against a surprise air attack on the grounds that it conflicted with our national traditions and brought to mind Pearl Harbor. Eventually the view prevailed that the less risky course, the quarantine, should be pursued initially; stronger actions could be commenced later should they become necessary. Kennedy moved the blockade as close to Cuba as he dared so that Khrushchev would have time to consider all the implications it presented. After some indecision the Kremlin decided to respect the blockade; as soon as the first ship with launching equipment turned away, the world was safe—for a time. Kennedy had heightened the confrontation by refusing Khrushchev's offer to remove the missiles if we would dismantle our own obsolete ones in Turkey. A diplomatic settlement was worked out whereby Russia removed all missiles from Cuba, and America promised to respect that country's territorial integrity. Some critics have faulted Kennedy for making the missile confrontation a public affair. He might have given Khrushchev a private ultimatum. Public exposure gave the Russian leader an opportunity to appear temperate in the face of world opinion. But Kennedy had grown beyond the Bay of Pigs affair, gaining courage and restraint.

It is said that the missile crisis scared Khrushchev; in the condescending vocabulary of the Chief of Staff Maxwell Taylor, it made him "tractable." It undoubtedly scared Kennedy, too. But the missile crisis, which might have blown up the world, instead cleared the air. A sudden realization dawned that in an age of national revolutionary movements such as Castro's Cuba, direct nuclear confrontation was no longer thinkable. Nineteen sixty-three was to be the year of the great international thaw. The United States and the Soviet Union, locked in nuclear stalemate, established a "hot line" to guard against future misunderstandings. In June the President delivered a moving speech at American University, calling for a new era of harmony and mutual progress with Russia. The Test Ban Treaty of 1963, which Kennedy drove through the Senate in face of stiff opposition from the Pentagon, was his one great positive accomplishment in foreign policy. The Soviets broke with the Chinese on the issue of peaceful coexistence and publicly stressed the need to avoid nuclear war, while the United States made arrangements to sell wheat to Russia. Kennedy himself was said to be tiring of Dean Rusk's clichéd rhetoric and hard-line ideas. In the long run, the missile crisis perhaps simply quickened the shift of the Cold War from confrontation between the superpowers to less cataclysmic "wars of national liberation," but the immediate effect was a loosening of tension.

On other issues as well, Kennedy began his presidential years unimpressively, and matured only as experience and circumstances compelled. Sobered by his meager margin of victory in 1960, he had arranged harmony meetings with Nixon and Eisenhower even before taking office, and he gave continuity to government (and continued conservative policies) by keeping on officials such as J. Edgar Hoover of the FBI and Allen Dulles of the CIA. After Congress convened in 1961 Kennedy forced a change in the size of the House Rules Committee, and thereby opened up the possibility that controversial legislation might at least reach the floor. But again his margin of victory was so slight that in the months ahead he rarely challenged Congress on important issues: federal aid to education floundered on religious controversy; a new cabinet department of urban affairs failed to win approval; foreign aid was cut drastically, owing to successive administration blunders. The Trade Expansion Act of 1962 was the one early achievement, but it was not of major importance, despite the publicity given it. Kennedy, it seemed, would endorse Jefferson's dictum: "Great innovations should not be forced on slender majorities."

The lack of programs of Kennedy's first year in the presidency is especially to be noted with respect to the great domestic issue of the sixties, the one for which he is honored most—that of civil rights. Actually, the President entered office with an undistinguished record on the question of race. Twice he had voted with the South on the Civil Rights Bill of 1957: on the abortive effort to return the bill to Mississippi Senator James Eastland's Judiciary Committee; and on the successful O'Mahoney amendment guaranteeing jury trials in criminal contempt cases—and so ensuring, in effect, that southern white defendants in civil rights cases would be tried by southern white juries. In the vice-presidential balloting of 1956 Kennedy had received support from such sources as Arkansas Governor Orville Faubus, and in the late fifties the governors of Alabama and Mississippi had urged his presidency. At a time when Kennedy was giving no more account of himself than this, Richard Nixon was calling for a strong civil rights bill and speaking against discrimination in jobs and housing.

Kennedy's campaign of 1960 was also unpromising on the question. When in January he listed the "real issues of 1960," he omitted civil rights—and this from a candidate who during the campaign declared, quoting Franklin D. Roosevelt, that the presidency is "above all, a place of moral leadership." Along with Nixon he did make many campaign promises to the cause of racial equality, and he even phoned a message of consolation to Mrs. Martin Luther King, whose husband had been imprisoned in an Atlanta jail. Dr. King's early release was probably attributable to a phone call from Robert Kennedy to an Atlanta judge. But in his inaugural President Kennedy mentioned civil rights only briefly and in the most general terms.

Fearing loss of support for other programs, Kennedy sponsored virtually no new rights legislation in 1961 and 1962, relying instead on executive action. He did not appear to sense the explosive potential of the racial situation. Had he understood it better, he would never have appointed his brother Attorney General, for that office bore the responsibility of enforcing civil rights laws, and it would have been politically astute to choose for it a man of independent reputation.

Yet the Department of Justice brought about much of the concrete gains the Kennedy administration achieved on racial matters. Believing that once southern Negroes voted, their political power would secure other rights, Bobby Kennedy introduced many new federal lawsuits in behalf of the Negro franchise. The Justice Department also saw to it that transportation facilities became almost entirely desegregated in the South. (In 1962, however, the Federal Aviation Agency awarded a $2 million grant to build an airport with segregated restaurants and rest rooms in Jackson, Mississippi.) Though he had earlier urged the Negro leader Ralph Abernathy to hold back the freedom riders, the Attorney General in May 1961 dispatched 600 federal marshals to Alabama to protect them. Vice-President Lyndon Johnson, who chaired the Committee on Equal Employment, took another approach: intimate with the art of persuasion, he urged government contractors to hire more Negro workers. But Johnson came to realize that coercion would be needed, and in 1963 the Vice-President delivered strong civil rights speeches in Gettysburg and Detroit.

President Kennedy avoided the ultimate sanction, that of forcing desegregation by the withholding of federal funds. In the fall of 1962, two years after criticizing Eisenhower for failing, "by a stroke of the presidential pen," to eliminate discrimination in federally assisted housing, the President did issue such an order, sandwiching it between major news releases so that it received minimal publicity; but administrative interpretations then softened even this forward step. President Kennedy decried "straight-from-the-shoulder platitudes" on civil rights, not comprehending that this was a place where presidential exhortation might be of some value. Whatever progress the Justice Department made in 1961 and 1962, the President wiped out some of it by appointing several segregationists to lifetime positions on southern district courts; they exhibited little enthusiasm for enforcing the Supreme Court school desegregation decision of 1954.

Then, in the last year of his life, Kennedy—and the churches and much of the nation—awakened to the moral crisis that the civil rights movement had long been seeking to publicize. Events compelled him to act, but he acted in a manner that brought credit to his presidency. In the fall of 1962 he had enforced with federal troops the enrollment of James Meredith at the University of Mississippi, employing radio and television to call on southerners to obey the law. The following spring, when Governor George Wallace attempted to prevent the court-ordered entrance of Vivian Malone and James Hood into the University of Alabama, the President's pronouncement went beyond the issue of obedience to law, where federal declarations in crises of illegal resistance to integration had typically placed themselves, and spoke to the moral question. (Earlier, Kennedy had borrowed Lincoln's birthday from the Republicans by inviting several hundred Negro leaders to the White House.) In May of 1963 Kennedy moved in troops to quell brutal repression in Birmingham, Alabama, where police had used dogs, fire hoses, and electric cattle prods against Negroes. In June he gave a moving speech on civil rights and he finally sent new legislation to Congress. The President proposed a limited ban on discrimination in public places, asked for powers enabling the Justice Department to sue for school desegregation where an aggrieved citizen asked its help, and urged a broad provision authorizing the government to withhold funds for federally assisted programs where discrimination occurred. But it contained no proposal for mandatory fair employment practices and failed to resurrect the unsuccessful Part III of the 1957 bill giving the Justice Department power to intervene in all civil rights cases. Kennedy also took a step backward when he gave tax reform priority over civil rights legislation, reasoning that a stronger economy would help the Negro more than anything else. And certainly the President feared southern congressional power. Some critics even charged that there was an unstated agreement with the South, gaining votes on other bills in exchange for stalling on civil rights. But just before he was killed the President secured an agreement from congressional leaders that would probably have assured passage of a strong civil rights act early in 1964.

Kennedy's claim to be celebrated as a champion of Negro rights is precarious. Though the great Negro leader, the Reverend Martin Luther King, Jr., granted in June 1963 that Kennedy had perhaps done "a little more" than Eisenhower, King added that "the plight of the vast majority of Negroes remains the same." The following August 250,000 people participated in the March on Washington to be counted in favor of civil rights legislation and to hear King speak: "I have a dream that one day on the red hills of Georgia the sons of former slaves and the sons of former slaveowners will be able to sit together at the table of brotherhood. . . . I have a dream that one day even the State of Mississippi, a desert state sweltering with the heat of injustice and oppression, will be transformed into an oasis of freedom and justice. . . . I have a dream that one day the State of Alabama . . . will be transformed into a situation where little black boys and black girls will be able to join hands with little white boys and girls and walk together as sisters and brothers." Despite Kennedy's failure to share King's vision, in few places did his death arouse such sorrow as in the Negro communities. And subsequent efforts to pass effective legislation gained from being construed as a memorial to the martyred President; the first law easily went through Congress early in 1964 and soon others followed.

The pattern of initiative in race relations during the Kennedy years generally repeated itself in the President's handling of the economy. Kennedy in the 1960 campaign had criticized the Republicans for not maintaining a high rate of economic growth and for lapsing into recessions from fear of employing advanced economic policies. In office, however, the new President at first proceeded cautiously, endorsing in practice the economic policies he had earlier condemned. Unemployment remained substantial in 1961 and 1962. Certainly many real obstacles held Kennedy back from economic experimentation: the adverse balance of payments discouraged expansive policies; a severe break in the stock market in May 1962 evoked distrust of the President in the economic community; he was wary of the image of "reckless spender" that the Republicans had tried to fix on the Democrats; and the congressional seniority system rewarded conservatives of long service. Kennedy did succeed in holding down the cost of living, and in 1961 he supported a boost in Social Security payments and the minimum wage to end the "Eisenhower recession" of 1960–1961. These techniques were similar to those Eisenhower himself had used when the economy faltered.

Kennedy evidently believed in such tools as deficit spending, a tax cut, and easy credit, but he thought the powerful and independent Federal Reserve Board might rebel at a novel program. But when the economy later in 1962 ceased its recovery from the earlier recession, the President and his able Republican Treasury Secretary, Douglas Dillon, decided to follow a truly radical economic policy. For the first relatively prosperous time in American history an administration proposed the deliberate unbalancing of the budget through tax reduction as a means of stimulating growth. It was a great victory for the university economists who had sought to influence the President. According to Ted Sorenson, Kennedy became convinced by a speech they prepared for him to deliver at the Economic Club of New York in December. He also believed that a tax cut was an indirect means of helping the poor, the black, and the cities—and the stock market, which had moved downward the preceding spring. If the tax policy should give new life to the economy, Congress might do something to redress the imbalance between public squalor and private affluence. Early in 1963 Kennedy proposed a $10 billion tax cut, despite a record-breaking peacetime deficit. The unbalanced budget troubled the business community, but it disliked high taxes even more and supported the President. After the Kennedy recommendations became law early in 1964, the pace of economic growth quickened, and before our extensive involvement in Vietnam, prosperity without serious inflation briefly seemed within reach. In a sense, then, it was Kennedy's tax policy, which led to a $30 billion enlargement of Gross National Product, that made possible the harvest of Great Society legislation.

Businessmen generally responded well to the economic policies of the Kennedy-Johnson years, though many of them continued to distrust the government's sympathy toward labor. Kennedy obtained tax credits and a liberal depreciation allowance for business in 1962, and reduced corporate income taxes by 20 percent in 1963. But he soon found himself in a confrontation with a powerful segment of business. Early in the Kennedy administration, which had vigorously pursued an anti-inflation policy, the steel industry attempted to raise prices. The act was a major embarrassment for the government, for when Labor Secretary Arthur Goldberg, anxious to avoid a critical strike that might delay economic recovery, had employed his experience in negotiation to persuade labor to keep its wage demands down, he had repeated an assurance given by industry leaders that prices would be held steady. When Roger Blough, President of U.S. Steel, appeared at the White House at 5:45 P.M. on April 10, 1962, to announce that press releases of an industry-wide price rise were just then being distributed, the President was furious. He quoted his father as having said that steelmen were "sons of bitches," and then launched an almost unprecedented attack on a major American industry. The President withdrew defense contracts and threatened antitrust action and new antitrust laws; he used every major branch of the government to bring the steel companies into line. Secretary of Commerce Luther Hodges, himself a businessman, gave Kennedy full support. The President addressed the people bluntly: "In this serious hour in our nation's history, when we are confronted with grave crises in Berlin and Southeast Asia . . . , the American public will find it hard, as I do, to accept a situation in which a tiny handful of steel executives whose pursuit of private power and profit exceeds their sense of public responsibility can show such utter contempt of the interests of 185 million Americans." Kennedy overplayed by having the FBI take some uncertain role, but by and large it was a handsome demonstration of presidential power in the service of the public interest. Big Steel, following the lead of some smaller companies, rescinded the price increase. Arthur Krock observed afterward that presidential anger "must be reserved for those rare occasions when the office and the nation as well as the man are basically offended"; the steel episode was such an occasion.

Made confident by successes in foreign affairs and hopeful of improving domestic life, Kennedy gave promise by 1963 of fashioning a stronger presidency. Then Kennedy, two years and ten months after becoming President, went to Dallas. In a typical but foolish gesture, the President sat in an open car moving slowly through the streets of the hostile southern city. In the previous presidential campaign, even Lyndon Johnson had been spat upon in Dallas, and a woman had hit Ladybird on the head with a placard. And only weeks before, Adlai Stevenson had been physically abused there. The man who almost certainly shot and killed Kennedy, Lee Harvey Oswald, was a refugee of the political Left; but he might easily have been a right-wing fanatic or any lunatic with a grudge against the government. The President's body was flown home to Washington, where the next day, November 23, 1963, a Roman Catholic mass was held in the White House for the first time—something bigots had feared. Chief Justice Earl Warren, reporting swiftly for an investigation panel of eminent but busy men, uncovered no evidence of a conspiracy, and subsequent efforts to find one have proved unconvincing.

A summary view of the Kennedy administration would be out of focus if it concentrated heavily on how much legislation passed through Congress. Such a view could not take into account the times and the might-have-beens—or the possibility that the death of Kennedy provided the national temper needed for the passage of the Kennedy program. This is not to say that the domestic achievements of the thousand days were unimpressive. When Kennedy promised in the presidential campaign to get the country moving again he was referring principally to the economy. As a result of Kennedy's recommendations, the national economy became brilliantly active. Kennedy's belated leadership in the civil rights movement must not be discounted. But the President also made the White House a home for the arts, and he even promised that America would reach the moon before the decade was finished. Important legislation surmounted the congressional deadlock of the early sixties, including the Peace Corps and drug labeling; and critical beginnings were made on problems of water and air pollution, area redevelopment, and manpower training. Finally, Kennedy acted intelligently in crises: Ole Miss, the University of Alabama, Birmingham, the steel episode, the Cuban missile crisis, and—at least by refusing to compound errors—the Bay of Pigs.

What made the Kennedy years most memorable, besides the event that brought them to a premature conclusion, was something quite intangible. The ambiance of the administration was more significant than its actual legislative record. In attempting to answer various social needs that the New Deal had failed to meet and that had enlarged and multiplied in twenty years of political stasis during hot and cold war, President Kennedy implied that the country could no longer simply go its ordinary way. It required a more intense and faster pace, and a call to moral arms—in the rhetoric of the campaign, a "new frontier." John and Jacqueline Kennedy placed a high and racy fashion of living before a people of growing affluence. It can be granted that much of the Kennedy style fed upon glittering, banal values, that the President's record displays naiveté as often as sophistication, that Kennedy's own taste was often trivial and dull, and that estimates of him are colored by his romance with the intellectuals. But the Kennedy manner gave sharper edge to American life, created expectations still unfulfilled, gave encouragement to civil rights workers, and contributed something to an awakening among America's youth.

Certain forces of the Kennedy era were moving toward a fundamental reconsideration of American society. The issues here are hard to characterize: broadly speaking, they are cultural rather than economic; they relate to race, education, health, the environment, public safety, attitudes toward youth and the quality of life. They are founded, most of them, in the economic and social concern that American liberalism has carried down from the New Deal. The emergence of the racial question in the Kennedy years, however, would bring radical acts of civil disobedience and militant protest by the young, as well as new strivings for social reconstructions and innovative conceptions of community. A cultural politics, which the President scarcely intended, was spawned in the Kennedy years.

a liberal society

Chapter Three Both the initial expectations of the 1960s and the
ultimate distress of the decade were directed
toward liberalism: the liberal culture that the Kennedy administration represented with so much pa-
nache, the liberal programs that Lyndon Johnson
pursued with such effectiveness, the liberal foreign
policy that came to such a denouement in Asia, the
liberal scholarship that the universities and foundations supported, the liberal aid and often the leadership that black Americans once accepted and then
found an affliction. America was a liberal civilization in the sixties as it had been a business civilization in the twenties; not everyone was a liberal,
not everyone accepted liberal values, but liberalism
offered the style that the citizen took or rejected,
provided the heroes and then the scapegoats. Any
understanding of American culture in the age has to
begin with the amorphous entity known as American liberalism.

In pursuit of very general ideals—intellectual freedom, equality before the law, and the progressive amelioration of social ills—liberals in this country have advocated many and differing policies in the past century. Liberalism is not a creed or a utopian image of a future society. It is simply the body of values, experience, and aspiration possessed by a special social group. Just as American conservatism is the ideology of the American business community, and looks to business institutions to direct the nation's progress, liberalism is the attitude of the men who staff the cultural apparatus created by an industrial society, and who would entrust the national future to the institutions of journalism, education, and the reform movements they create or absorb.

Modern American liberalism had its beginnings in the colleges and press of the nineteenth century. Its characteristic product was the reform or public opinion journal such as *The Nation* or *Harper's Weekly*, journalism for college-educated men. Its most important practitioners have been academics and journalists. These two institutions, the college and the press of the nineteenth century, gave American liberalism a method and style still detectable in the present day. The liberal mind has always been a journalistic mind, fixed on the present even when studying the past, poking around closets, raking in mud, uncovering dirty secrets. The press was a natural vehicle for reformers who put their trust in an orderly political and social process conducted amidst rational public discussion; the colleges conveyed to liberalism the flavor of nineteenth-century American culture, which looked generally to the moral rather than the esthetic question, and which cast human suffering into the form of pathos, responding to it with sentiment and indignation. Down to the present, the enemies of liberalism will characteristically accuse it of self-righteousness and a "bleeding heart," while its clients will adopt its own moralistic standards to condemn liberals for power politics that would be accepted from any other group in American society.

In the twentieth century, liberals added to journalism and moralism the ideal of science. The new social sciences came to apply the scientific method—in such forms as statistical analysis and psychological testing—to the masses of information presented by an increasingly sophisticated journalism; and liberal economists, political scientists, and sociologists, as well as lawyers, administrators, and social workers influenced by them, began to assume the journalistic functions of investigation, of ferreting out hardship and abuse, of discovering or creating the news. Through the instrumentalities of science, liberals were able to relate directly to the central productive processes of the age, especially so as scientific research in universities brought business into parts of the academic community. Liberal journalism, of course, had been directly a part of the business community even when critical of it. The result was an instance of the "antagonistic cooperation" or "cooperative competition" that social scientists have found to be the normal relation among groups in American society. Liberalism and business, frequently hostile in philosophy and often violently critical of each other, also continued to exist in reciprocal dependence.

Historically, liberals have not constituted a definable interest group. Until recently, the cultural apparatus was far too small, involved too few people, and failed to differentiate liberals sufficiently from other members of the middle class. The liberals who have championed the ideal of a pluralism among interest groups, each pressing its own practical cause, as the best avenue to an otherwise undefinable general interest, have not lived by the code, for they have always seen other people's interests as more solid and demanding than their own. The role of the liberals has been custodial: the attempt to care for the dispossessed and to teach the middle class its responsibilities through the investigation of problems, the pointing of their moral import, and the suggestion of policies to remedy them. The moral strength provided by this absence of an articulate self-interest is obvious enough, yet custodianship also carries its own moral jeopardy. The liberal could confuse his tastes or his romantic projections with the real needs of others in situations of which he had no experience. Oscar Handlin tells of a social worker who complained of Italians who were not yet Americanized—they were still eating spaghetti. At the same time, the liberal could become dependent upon his clients, whose existence gives him purpose and direction, and he could turn his custodianship into a paternalism that is direct and offensive. Eldridge Cleaver has written that after Lyndon Johnson proclaimed "We shall overcome," no self-respecting Negro could ever again use the expression. Liberalism, in sum, holds a great potential for demoralization.

The last few decades have wrought an important change in the character of liberalism. The intelligentsia in which it subsists, once a scattering of professionals and free-lance people, has become a large coherent establishment, and its philosophy has come to reflect not only a moral instinct but concrete interests. Every need of modern society breeds this new group. Depression, war, and finally the Cold War and the permanent welfare state created the demand for a vastly enlarged federal bureaucracy, a huge enterprise in gathering statistics, charting policy, and engineering social change. Many of the new bureaucrats, whatever their background or partisan interests, performed the classic liberal labors of organizing intelligence to direct social change. And even the private economy became totally dependent on them, as, for one thing, government took over from the faltering business and financial world the task of managing the level of investment and saving. Under stress of an extraordinary development in the technology of weapons and unprecedented policy problems, the military soon developed its own intelligentsia. A similar element gathered as rapidly in private business to undertake its elaborate work in management and planning and to fill its special needs in public relations and industrial psychology.

All these specialists relied on a further extension of the new class. Modern government and business could not exist without the mass media. Advertising provides the nexus between the consumer and the productive process; and the citizen is connected to his government by electronic communications as he once was by oratory, political clubs, and favors. And so we have a large special segment of the intelligentsia working in information, both words and images.

The major beneficiaries of all this have been the agencies of education. As automobiles were the main growth industry and dominant influence in the direction of the economy during the first part of the century and government services and weaponry in the middle years, so education has become dominant and, despite its present financial crisis, is likely to remain so for the rest of the century. The expansion in the need throughout the economy for technical and professional expertise has been one reason, and the presence of a large intellectual class committed to education and ambitious for its children's schooling is another. But the strongest single financial force has been the government, which has become the great patron of modern science. Physics was the master discipline all during the period in which atomic weapons were being developed, but mathematics, especially in relation to computers, was increasingly important. The global reach of recent foreign policy has been a spur to investment in both natural and social science. Gain in the life sciences and agronomy reflected our commitment to world economic development, population control, and public health. The venture into space brought funding for further needs in metallurgy, medicine, systems analysis, and computer technology, as well as astronomy, solid state physics, and chemistry. The social sciences grew nearly as profusely. Data about every part of the world became vital, and people who had once considered themselves specialists in esoteric civilizations suddenly found their opinions sought in Washington and by the mass media. Political science profited, as did history, anthropology, and sociology. It was a good time to be young and in graduate school; every year the student heard of new fields for which money was becoming available, much of it from the federal government. The support brought prominence to the graduate school, which set the standards throughout the educational system and constituted a crucial link with the bureaucracies in government and industry that shared with it the burgeoning technologies.

An alliance of government and the weapons industry dominated the economic system in the fifties, setting directions for the collaboration of government and science; but in the late fifties, attacks on this interlocking system as a threat to democracy and peace (and for its economic artificiality) gathered force, and they foreshadowed its end. The percentage of government funds going directly into weapons came to a peak in the early sixties. Thereafter, it was education and research themselves, still drawing in part on weapons money, that promised the greatest economic growth and social return on investment, supplying the men and women whose special skills were as central to the new technology as land had been to the agricultural society and capital to early industrialism.

The intelligentsia was now a large and aggressive group, wielding powerful institutions and disciplines, concerned like every other element in society to capture its share of government policy. In recent years it has sought civilian control of technology, and government support for education, science, the arts, and the amenities of life; it has a taste for highways clear of billboards, clean air and water, good schools, and cultural centers.

All this has meant a change in the tenor of liberalism, but one that is subtle and at most half-conscious. The intellectual liberals have seldom realized that their demands now involve self-interest as well as the altruistic morality of custodianship, which they certainly retain. While their pleasure during the Kennedy years at being, so it seemed, an important part of a governmental coalition was grounded in some of the same ambitions for security and power as those that move organized labor or the farm vote, or any other group not at all guilt-ridden at the quest, they would argue honestly that they wanted power for the good social uses they could make of it. Though their cultural and ecological programs reflect their personal discomfort at living amidst mediocrity and ravaged surroundings, they have wished to rescue their fellow citizens too. They have presumed that their interests encompass the entire society, much as agrarian spokesmen in the nineteenth century and business leaders of the first half of the twentieth century had done before them. And the emergence of civil rights early in the decade into primacy among liberal issues, along with the commanding presence of custodial liberalism in the person of John F. Kennedy, represented a persistence of the old altruism that has made it even more difficult to see the harder side to liberalism.

Liberal aspirations lifted, at the beginning of the decade, with the great vigor of the productive and economic process. They have been connected to the process in many ways: its technology is the embodiment of the rational intelligence that liberalism has espoused; it is manned by technicians and planners some of whom represent or come under the influence of the liberal intelligentsia; and in the mid-sixties it was supplying, smoothly and abundantly, the means for the accomplishment of daring liberal programs, while its successes were bringing prestige to the social sciences. For an instant, liberalism and the productive forces came into a splendid union, to be followed by major frustration.

Beyond almost any previous time in American history, the sixties were an era of expectancy. The future will find it difficult to recapture the sense that this pungent period exuded. Many Americans looked for the full integration of Negroes into American life without violence or serious disruption of older patterns outside the South. The remarkable progress that the black man made during the decade invited the prediction that a wrong of four hundred years, and its products, would quickly become extinct. Americans thought that the age of economic insecurity, the only age the masses of the world have known in historical times, was now behind them. Their spending patterns, especially their willingness to incur debt, all attest to this attitude. A particularly fit image of it was the stock market, an organized market in expectations. It was not the bull market of the twenties, conveying the hopes of private wealth to a segment of the middle class. It was the funds of union pensions, the assets of universities (seldom before invested in common stocks), and mutual funds—the pooled savings of the millions. The expectations were blunted after 1968, but not subject to the collapse that the dreams of the twenties had produced.

The expectations go back to a real achievement, the economic boom engineered by the "new economics," the longest by far in American history. Perhaps more than anything else, this boom convinced many Americans—and most leaders of opinion and politics—that man was able to engineer the social circumstances he wanted. It was, wrote Daniel P. Moynihan, "perhaps the most impressive demonstration that has yet occurred . . . of the capacity of organized intelligence to forecast and direct events." And the new economics proved its magical properties by working through tax cuts. It was an economic order in which progress, created by a lowering of taxes, actually increased the tax revenues and through them paid for governmental programs of rich benefit to the citizens; and it attracted virtually everyone, even the conservatives whose belief in balanced budgets was no match for their desire for low taxes.

The social sciences got much of the honor, and the liberals set them to enormous work. There was great confidence in the ability of social scientists to effect planned change. The best illustration was the amount of money spent on social science research, most of it in projects of immediate social relevance. Part of the euphoria surrounding race relations came from the belief that with enough money scientific means could be found to overcome nearly anything. The Head Start program of the mid-sixties was an early venture; technological teaching aids were a major weapon still being used today; and most ambitious of all was the "community action program," designed to engineer the very existence of a community.

Insofar as private citizens thought about their large investment in the social sciences and the programs of the Great Society, they considered it an investment in problem solving. Some of the liberal social planners shared that naive faith, in fact believing that if everyone else would only stay out of their way and let their work progress, we would be projected into a new "techneutronic" age. Social scientists are supposed to be trained, however, to look at things quite differently, to know as pure scientists know that actions are experimental, uncertain in outcome, and that any project however good has much error and wasted energy to it. Many of the social technicians therefore realized quite clearly that the investment was in experimentation, and proceeded to work their experiments on the great social laboratory that the government was providing them, some with greater and others with less sensitivity and tact toward the human objects whose lives they were rearranging.

Projects of the Great Society were readily justified on their own experimental grounds, and they left not only a legacy of good accomplishment but also a precious body of data available in no other way, which will keep social scientists busy for a generation. Most of the shortcomings were of a sort predictable in advance. In enterprises of such scale, graft was inevitable. So was the "waste" of which conservatives liked to talk, for the programs were not working toward ends for which the means are immediately definable and available; they had to grope their way toward the solution of intangibles: the mysterious bonds of communities, the uncertain consequences of planned changes, the whole psychology of poverty.

Another problem might possibly have been controlled to an extent. The most visible injury that the liberal programs sustained was political. The poor were made impatient. The failure of progress convinced radicals that the Great Society was a sham. And the public was angry that its money went with so little visible return, and that some of the recipients had taken to rioting and black racism. Though we are still the restless, discontented people whom de Tocqueville encountered in 1830, we persist in seeing ourselves as the happy tenders of American gardens, at ease with our lot and the world, and the nation could not understand why black people, offered a change for improvement, did not become as contented as we imagine ourselves to be. Perhaps the planners could have made clear how very experimental the projects were, and prepared us to expect only partial success. This, however, would have cut against the millennial expectations that did much to call forth the programs and to make the nation willing to finance them.

The military intelligentsia and the technical managers of business both suffered a fate similar to that of the social scientists. The military had developed an expertise unparalleled in the history of warfare. Yet the sudden urgencies of Vietnam made military advisers forget their old cautions about a land war in Asia. When they found themselves in Southeast Asia, they began a series of experiments, each of which was hailed as the way to military success. When none found the elusive way, people talked of a credibility gap. There was some deliberate falsehood, but much of the trouble was the same problem the social scientists had discovered: that the technician unlearns as much as he learns in a mass experimental situation, that he must appear sure in order to be given the means to experiment, but that he really does not know.

Business and its experts had some of the pressure off them in the decade. The old notion of business leadership toward the eradication of poverty and the provision of a secure middle-class existence for all Americans had been shattered in the Great Depression, and its revival in the fifties had been brief and incomplete. Government, it was assumed by the sixties, had the final responsibility for the operation of the economy. Business simply worked in its given sphere, providing its marvelous private goods. And in the sixties, business provided more of them. Dullness and standardization were no longer typical complaints. Everything came in a dozen models and more shades. Esoteric goods were now available even in the mail-order catalogues, and the sophistication of the consumer grew by a great if unmeasurable factor.

But slowly through the decade, and more rapidly as it ended, disturbing results appeared from this latest and furthest elaboration of the old American penchant for gadgets. The new laundry presoaks were deadly pollutants. The cars, so Ralph Nader demonstrated, were full of safety flaws. Telephones came in several shapes and all colors, but increasingly they did not work. In 1965 the New York City area suffered a giant power failure. The worsening air, much of it due to the high compression automobile engines and the huge demand for electric power, stirred all the organs of publicity into action. The situation in New York City was perhaps the worst in the country, and there lay the center of the communications industry. The result was that Americans soon heard endlessly about the power gap and the pollution problem. There was talk of the greedy men who had allowed things to arrive at such terrible proportions. But again, although greed certainly had its part in the story, the main culprit was clearly the imperfections of technology, the inability of the engineers to plan for all the factors affecting demand and all the consequences of enlarged facilities and new methods. Once more, the expectations for technological utopia had proved excessive, and left behind resentments and distrust of major institutions.

Perhaps the most massive hope of the decade was in education. In the sixties, the nation moved from the high school to the multiversity. Much has been written about the discontents of the college student, but what of the citizens who supported their universities so nobly and then seemed to turn on them with so much passion? The reaction went beyond distaste for the student culture and turned into a general taxpayers' revolt against the university system as a whole. In part, it became a question of finances. In the time of great expectation, people had not quite calculated on paying for higher schooling; instead they had looked to the new campuses to create jobs, raise land values, cure social problems, and so enrich the community that the initial cost would be absorbed. Some of this came true. But the expansive economy that provided the means for the schools and got further health from them also militated against their support, which became a strain upon the bursting, credit-laden budgets of the citizenry.

The new economists, in fact, were ambivalent on the question of public spending. Even as they welcomed it, and persuaded citizens of its beneficence, they encouraged the accumulation of expensive private goods in the absence of efficient public services. A few people drank bottled water; everyone traveled in his own car. People cleaned their own air with air purifiers or air conditioners (whose power requirements added to the dirt of the outside air), and purchased their own recreation. For all the official liberalism of the era, the sixties did much to nourish the traditional privatism of American culture. The technology that Marshall McLuhan claimed was bringing us together into a "global village" also had the potential for the further isolation of the individual.

Liberalism, business, and technology drew together in the sixties through their common commitments to rationality and technique. Economic success temporarily quieted old quarrels between liberalism and business, and amidst the prosperity a burgeoning class of technicians was able to pursue expansive social goals. Their moment of large achievement in the sixties leaves an important legacy. Nevertheless, the cost to liberalism must be measured as well. Radicals claimed with some truth that liberalism was no longer distinguishable from America's established powerful institutions. Essentially, it had implicated itself in all the forces that it had once considered its main enemies: the corporations, the military, and the local self-isolated elites of wealth and power and profession who were defending their elegant private way of life against the encroachments of the industrial society their own institutions guided. The self-interest of the classes that were speaking for liberalism, and the particular social and institutional arrangements to which it had allied itself, together made impossible its traditional role of speaking for a wide and diffuse ethical impulse within American life. Liberals learned that their desires were not always identical with the aims of the whole nation, that their methods were also often misunderstood or rejected, and that their values could not spread to other groups in society. They were now alone in an America that liberalism had done heroic work in creating.

Lyndon Baines Johnson rounds up a steer on a visit to his Texas ranch, 1964. (Wide World)

U.S. Marines and Army personnel set up a roadblock in Santo Domingo during the Dominican Republic rebellion, May 1965. (Pictorial Parade)

Appalachia. (Paul Conklin)

the war on poverty

A VISTA volunteer in the South. (Ken Heyman)

A VISTA worker visits an Appalachian family. (Ken Heyman)

LBJ at a Job Corps Center in San Marcos, Texas. (UPI)

New Mexico. (Marcia Keegan)

A Navajo, and his hogan in the background. (Paul Conklin)

A doctor from the Department of Health examines Indian children. (Ken Heyman)

Republican presidential nominee, Senator Barry Goldwater, and his vice-presidential running mate, William Miller. Phoenix, Arizona, 1964. (UPI)

Senator Goldwater, 1964. (UPI)

President Johnson lifts Her, one of his pet beagles, on the White House grounds, 1964. (Wide World)

Democratic Convention, Atlantic City, 1964. (UPI)

the war in vietnam

(Pictorial Parade)

(UPI Radiophoto)

Fastest Gun by Roy Lichtenstein.
(Courtesy L. M. Asher Family, Los Angeles)

(Fred McDarrah)

(Shelly Rusten)

(Pictorial Parade)

(Tom McCarthy)

(Shelly Rusten)

March on the Pentagon,
October 1967. (Fred McDarrah)

Cost of living goes up, up, up.
(Wide World)

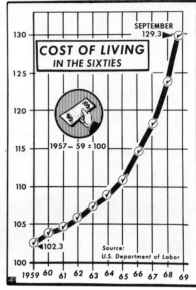

SEPTEMBER
129.3

COST OF LIVING
IN THE SIXTIES

130

125

120

115

110

105

100

1957 – 59 = 100

102.3

Source:
U.S. Department of Labor

1959 60 61 62 63 64 65 66 67 68 69

Ralph Nader and a staff member at Senate Auto Subcommittee Hearing, 1966. (UPI)

A team of heart specialists, headed by Dr. Michael DeBakey, performs a heart transplant operation at Houston, 1966. (UPI)

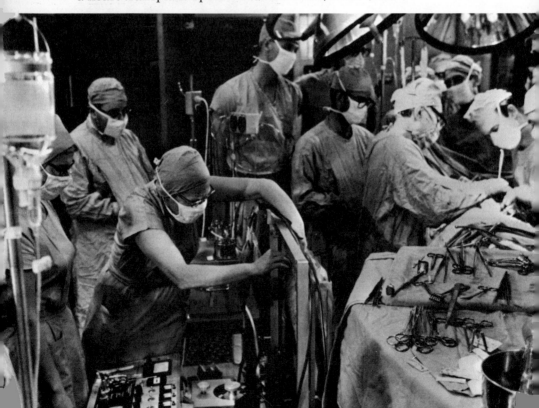

Astronauts Grissom, White, and Chaffee (l. to r.) at Cape Kennedy 10 days before they perished in an Apollo project training session. (Wide World)

Father Philip Berrigan and Rev. Daniel Berrigan watch draft board records burn after the records were taken from the Catonsville, Maryland, draft board office, 1968. (UPI)

The planet Earth seen from outer space.

(Wide World)

Presidential candidate Eugene McCarthy greets students at Tallahassee, Florida, 1968. (UPI)

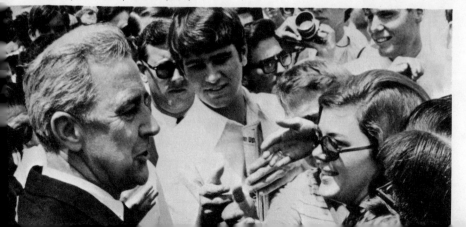

Senator Robert Kennedy, his family seated behind him, announces that he will challenge President Johnson in the race to the White House. Senate Caucus Room, March 1968. (Pictorial Parade)

Robert Kennedy campaigns on 12th Street in Detroit, Michigan, 1968. (Editorial Photocolor Archives)

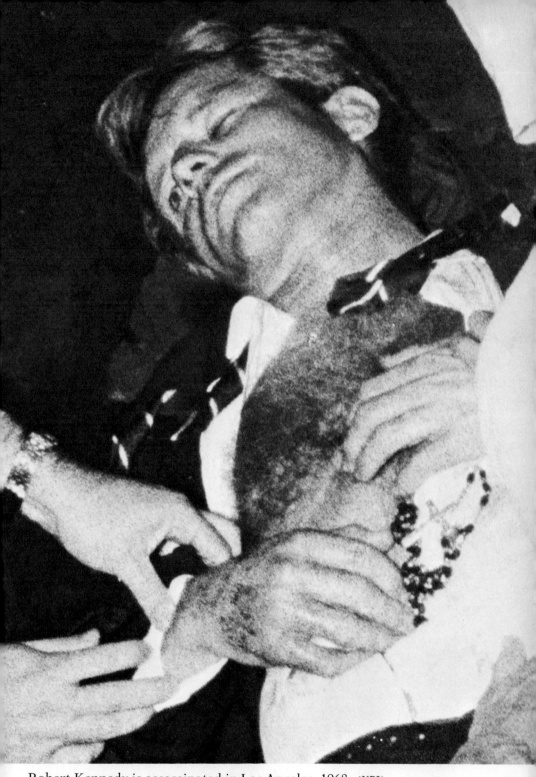
Robert Kennedy is assassinated in Los Angeles, 1968. (UPI)

Chicago Democratic Convention, 1968. (Fred McDarrah)

Mayor Daley responds to Senator Ribicoff, Chicago, 1968. (Wide World)

Senator Edward Kennedy—a dark horse at the 1968 Democratic Convention. (Richard Howard, Bethel)

Republicans rally at Madison Square Garden, 1968. (Richard Howard, Bethel)

Senator Edmund Muskie relinquishes the microphone, Washington, Pennsylvania, 1968. (UPI)

Senator Muskie campaigning in Portland, Oregon, 1968. (UPI)

Senator Hubert Humphrey leaves the polling booth, Marysville, Minnesota. (Pictorial Parade)

the civil rights movement

Chapter Four   John F. Kennedy represented a strain of liberalism
that easily entered into symbolic relationship with
black aspirations in the early sixties. Despite the
weakness of his own record on civil rights, Kennedy
represented a traditional custodial liberalism. The
language of responsibility, crisis, and social drama
came easily to him. Though the moral appeal of
the 1960 campaign had been thin, Kennedy's
inaugural address was alive with a moral fervor
that could not have been exceeded had the nation
been in the midst of civil turmoil or foreign war.
For all of liberalism's fastidiousness, its cool
rationalism, its devotion to science, and its care
for the legal forms that preserve men from their
own emotions and from one another, the liberal
conscience—even one as apparently cool as John
Kennedy's—has within it an unarticulated millennial vision, which leads it at some times into the

rankest sentimentalism and at others into confronting the deepest needs of society.

The civil rights movement provided an object for liberal solicitude, a moral edge to liberal emotions, and a justification for liberal power that fitted the traditional image of moral custodianship, free from the many ambivalences that would come to torment liberalism later in the decade. The movement under Martin Luther King, Jr., and his young followers was exactly fitted to command the imagination of liberalism. It was formal in a curious and gracious way, waging revolution in the cause of the law, and executing with restraint and precision its limited acts of civil disobedience. In its abjurations of hatred it seemed almost obsessively watchful over the quality of its feelings. And it was, so it appeared at instants, a community of grace, with powerful appeal to the central tendency of American religious history, the search for the Kingdom of God on earth. It renewed the liberal tendencies in American religion, providing the first important social content to the churches after their great numerical expansion in the preceding years.

The civil rights movement was both powerful and fragile. It had behind it the force of law and the potential power of the federal government. Beyond that it had peculiar moral strength resting on a rare combination of circumstances. Part of this force came from its unique opportunity at once to violate local ordinance and to uphold the national law. There is a special Christian symbolism in peaceful disobedience, though it is a symbolism in precarious antinomian relation to Christian orthodoxy. It can mean not only martyrdom, but also the witness of love against statute, of the New Testament against the rules of the Pharisees. And since, on the other hand, the laws against which civil disobedience was directed had been declared or were presumed to be unconstitutional, and some of the private discriminatory practices were outlawed by federal statute, the activists were nearly free of the moral ambivalence inherent in the conscientious violation of law. The goals that civil disobedience pursued, moreover, had a dual appeal. They were simple and understandable: it was easy to identify with the desire for a meal at a lunch counter, a seat on a bus, a swim at a pool, the use of a library. Rarely in modern times has the ordinary had such dignity conferred upon it. And the goals were capable of instantaneous accomplishment. In a moment a lunch counter can be integrated, or a Negro seated at the front of a bus. The activists could do more than compel this kind of integration—in a very simple act of entering or sitting down, they could make it a fact. By its immediacy and clarity, integration of this sort implied the Christian drama of conversion; King urged that a man could throw off, in an instant, his racist past. A society at work training its poor for jobs, arranging for a better distribution of its people, or mixing and improving its schools—all goals of the movement—is engaging in the lengthy plodding tasks of moral common sense; but in the small gesture of stepping across an invisible line, a society might give outward sign of its regeneration.

For decades white liberals had provided money and personnel for civil rights organizations—the National Association for the Advancement of Colored People, founded in 1909, and later the Urban League and the Congress of Racial Equality (CORE). Integration would provide exactly the kind of social circumstance liberals could believe in, for it was their own: good education and an entrance into the salariat, the professions, and the government. White lawyers had fought alongside black in a series of court contests over segregation that culminated in the great Supreme Court decision of 1954 in *Brown* v. *Board of Education,* which declared segregated public schooling to be unconstitutional. The direct actionist movement that gained its first national attention with the Montgomery bus boycott of 1955 therefore compelled a response from liberalism.

The relation of liberalism to the movement was to be ambivalent. The young liberals who directly participated, and in their participation passed to the left of conventional politics, were perhaps clearest among the white youths as to what they were doing; their main confusion would come with the arrival of black nationalism. But as the incidence of disorder increased, there were others who looked on hopefully and wistfully, who worried over the excesses and mistakes. Their cautious regard for procedures and their fears over political consequences strained the patience of the activists. Or the estrangement came indirectly: rights workers simply entered upon a new experience and acquired a style that was outside the terms in which other Americans lived.

In February 1960 the movement turned into a major revolt when four black students from the North Carolina Agricultural and Technical College in Greensboro sat in at the local Woolworth's segregated lunch counter. The men who began the "second American Revolution" were even younger than the youthful revolutionaries of 1773. Ezell Blair, Jr., David Richmond, Franklin McCain, and Joseph McNeill were all freshmen, seventeen- and eighteen-year-olds, when they requested their cups of coffee on the afternoon of February 1. Their return the next day with sixteen fellow students brought national wire service attention. On the third day, they were fifty strong and they had been joined by a few white girls, students from the Women's College. On Friday the movement started to spread, to other stores and then to other cities.

The effect was electric. In an estimated 130 localities, whites, mostly students, demonstrated in support. Such major figures of the civil rights movement as Bob Moses, Julian Bond, James Forman, and John Lewis suddenly discovered their vocation in that exciting February; many other young people abandoned the passivity of the 1950s for a purposeful existence. The Congress of Racial Equality, organized and until 1961 led by whites, leapt into the movement, offering years of experience with nonviolent techniques of direct action, which the students readily took up.

The older civil rights groups and liberal forces rapidly followed, some enthusiastically, some with hesitancy over the tactic of direct action. The NAACP Legal Defense Fund proved to be the mainstay of the student movement, clearing at enormous expense and exertion the legal problems that the tactics were designed to create. In fact, the NAACP, later ritually denounced by the militants as an Uncle Tom organization, engaged extensively in direct action itself while continuing its more traditional work in litigation and lobbying. The Urban League, long the most conservative of the major civil rights organizations, became far more outspoken and powerful under its new leader, Whitney Young, Jr. And Martin Luther King, Jr., who could claim authorship of the student movement, rose to preeminence in the civil rights revolution. His Southern Christian Leadership Conference (SCLC) flourished, and he presided at the forming of the Student Nonviolent Coordinating Committee (SNCC), destined to be the strong left arm of the revolution for the next several years. Outside the movement, white liberal politicians as well as the directors of major foundations hastened to catch up with the advance guard.

None of this ought to be surprising. The students had set off a competition for leadership and for credits that is entirely understandable. In such circumstances, militancy itself is an advantage, just as in quieter ages consistency and patience are the assets. As expectations grow, whatever promises the most immediate results wins support. And the sit-ins did gain immediate results. These few years bubbled with illusion, but won massive accomplishment as well. Moral power did seem capable of overcoming evil. Genuine social progress did result, and the sense of identity among all the groups engaged in the struggle was strengthened in positive ways, for the blacks most of all, but also for their student allies, the liberal wing of the Democratic party, and the white churches.

What made these times so heady, so prolific of dangers and opportunities, was that this was one of the unusual moments when initiative could actually come upwards, from the ranks to the established leadership. "We don't need the adults," one of the youths at the NAACP convention in 1961 announced, "but they need us." The older leaders had talked courageously about integration and made firm beginnings for it, but they were Black Moses, pointing across the river at the promised land. They had fed their flock in the cruelest desert for more than the biblical forty years, but the mass integration for which they labored had never yet been seen. A nervous black man in a somber suit at a liberal party, or Jackie Robinson finally able to show his temper on a baseball field, was not the realization of a dream deferred. King had already shown that behind the careful legal strategies and the astute lobbying lay a millennial impulse demanding something more than modest gains and an end to the grossest indignities.

The young people of the civil rights revolution in those brief years crossed the river into the promised land. In retrospect they may appear to have walked on the water, so difficult does it seem now. The common cause and the common danger seemed capable of transforming old attitudes exactly as Martin Luther King said they should. For a white youth of a northern city to learn from a summer in Mississippi that white people were to be feared and black ones trusted was to unlearn his whole life's history, genuinely to solve the personal "Negro problem" that Norman Podhoretz has attributed to every white American. It was not the integrationist objectives of the movement that mattered most (when he was finally served at the lunch counter, Dick Gregory used to say, he discovered that the food was terrible), and some crucial ones were never realized; rather, the movement *was* integration. It kindled, briefly, a vision of a communal brotherhood that casts into shadow much in the nation's history. The possibilities those years raised that white and black might live together (or die together, like Andrew Goodman, James Chaney, and Michael Schwerner in Mississippi in 1964) will haunt the American psyche. But so too will the cracking of that fragile coalition.

"Movement" and "direct action" are crucial terms denoting the psychology that the Negro revolution released upon the decade. They were not clichés—not then. The revolution needed pace, an incessant sequence of confrontations and victories that would capture men and women of good will and impress the opposition with the resistlessness of the movement. The coverage given by the media sustained the impression. While all groups in American society were becoming more and more open to the medium of television as an instrument of persuasion and power, the young people had a particularly close if not always efficacious sense of it. Doubtlessly they were less deliberate in their use of it than many of their elders, but their methods suited it perfectly. Dramas of immediacy, the act or threat of violence from the opposition, the clear posing of moral issues in physical confrontations, all fitted the visual form in which the news was conveyed. Still, it would be inaccurate to attribute all the power of the demonstrations to the media: people must be responsive to the moral content of an incident or it will soon be forgotten. A century before, John Brown's raid had become known and felt almost as quickly, with as much emotion, as the acts of the civil rights workers.

The momentum continued into 1961 with the Freedom Rides. The Congress of Racial Equality, with the longest history of direct action, moved into the forefront with the appointment of James Farmer as its national director. Within three months after his appointment, he had organized and sent out groups to test racial discrimination in interstate travel. The riders, despite the rigid non-violent discipline they maintained, left behind them a long trail of violence, especially the burning of a bus by white segregationists in Anniston, Alabama. The major effect of the rides was to force the federal government into action. The Kennedy administration sent federal marshals into Alabama to protect the riders, and the Attorney General, Robert F. Kennedy, requested the Interstate Commerce Commission to ban segregation in interstate bus terminals. By November 1, the prohibition was in effect. It achieved immediate compliance in many places, and it was the beginning of a long process that within the decade would end virtually all discriminatory practice in public transportation.

The direct actionists by now were forcing the pace not only of the older civil rights leadership, but of the national government as well. The federal marshals of 1961 were followed by federal troops in 1962 at the University of Mississippi, where the governor of the state attempted to prevent James Meredith from enrolling as the first Negro student and then reneged on agreements with Washington to keep order with state troopers. In 1963 the federal government was forced to move from executive action to the support of new civil rights legislation, while the demonstrators were turning to larger and more dangerous targets in the deep South and now even in the North. The year 1963 was rich in symbolic fulfillments and practical frustrations for the civil rights movement and the nation. It marked an important turning point between a time of élan and the subsequent years of power and confusion for the movement that were to reach their climax in 1968.

The last field to which the activists rushed and the leadership followed was Birmingham, Alabama. What appeared to be a decision by Martin Luther King and the SCLC was in fact, by King's testimony, the product of the Reverend Fred Shuttlesworth's seven-year-old Birmingham organization, student boycotts in 1962, and rumors that the SCLC would enter the battle if agreements white businessmen had made with Shuttlesworth were not kept. With the local organization in danger and SCLC's credibility inadvertently involved in its success, King and his associates, in his words, "reached the conclusion that we had no alternative but to go through with our proposed . . . campaign."

The campaign faced difficulties from every side. The city was a bastion of segregation and the state governor, George Wallace, was moving into leadership of the segregation forces in the country. The black community of Birmingham was itself hesitant to engage in any radical action, fearing divisions in its own midst and lacking confidence in the ability of its leaders to control the black poor. And the state of the movement by 1963 had called forth increasing militancy. A few arrests no longer made an impression: the scale of activities would have to be massive, with all the dangers that suggested, especially since there seemed so little grounds for optimism over the possibility of achieving the local goals around which the movement would revolve.

What happened in Birmingham is vividly remembered: the fire hoses and the police dogs, the rioting and the bombings, the thousands in jail, and the dead children. Out of it occurred events that changed irrevocably the nature of the movement. The demonstrations touched the black community far beyond the reach of the civil rights leadership. Peaceful demonstration was met, as so often, with white violence, but now in response to white violence black crowds rose under no man's control. One thing that became apparent for the first time was the extent to which the success of the middle-class aims the revolution pursued had rested on the passivity of the ghetto blacks, who could not afford a meal in an integrated restaurant, who had no money to travel, and who thought too little about politics to be concerned about their right to vote. The period of urban rioting began in Birmingham. Not all Americans understood this, for they could still blame what happened on conditions peculiar to the South, but the President was prophetic. Proclaiming that demonstrations could no longer be conducted with order and safety, Kennedy raised the alarm on the "fires of frustration and discord . . . burning in every city, North and South," and called for a civil rights bill to end segregation in most "places of public accommodation." He had finally thrown the mantle of the national administration, the Democratic party, and the liberal community over the civil rights movement. Henceforth the generals would lead the troops. The time had arrived for practical activity in place of direct demonstration.

The result was a major effort to slow the direct actionists or to turn them in another direction, an effort that gradually met with substantial though never total success. The prospect of civil rights legislation was a motive for restraint, as were the threat from the Right in 1964 and the whole range of Great Society programs. The solid historic gains of the era came in these years. There were also reasons internal to the movement, bringing it, if not to a halt, at least to a fragmentation of its energies.

Techniques of direct action had largely reached their limits by 1963. They made sense only for the kinds of discrimination that could be ended immediately, and even these changes had proved possible only in localities where the Negro also constituted a political threat. In the deep South—in Orangeburg, in Baton Rouge, and in Jackson—the demonstrations had been failures. Even the Birmingham trouble, which had led to federal legislation, resulted at the time in only partial success for the local demands of the civil rights forces. Without voting strength such as the larger urban ghettos provided, there was no future in direct action, and some of the radicals, especially Bob Moses of SNCC in Mississippi, rapidly realized this. Yet the radicals who turned to voter registration (encouraged in many cases by support from white liberal foundations urged on by the administration) were, after all, doing little more than strengthening the Democratic party. Whatever they did, they directly served the cause of the national government, which was asking them to replace their demonstrations by orthodox political activity. Now the radicals were in the service of the moderates, applying pressure for them to use or even adding to their voting strength.

The urban North was also bounded in its possibilities. The year 1963 was the time when the demonstrations spread northward in force. They met with less direct resistance, but also less accomplishment. Demonstrations against discriminatory building trades unions and *de facto* segregation were fruitless. The ritual was inadequate: no instant capitulation was possible when the demands were complicated and the objectives gradual. The northern demonstrations, in fact, had a double handicap. Not only did they not succeed either practically or in cathartic satisfactions; they also threatened the liberal coalition that had now become the primary hope for ending segregation. The motives, from within and without, for at least a lull in the movement were overwhelming.

On the other hand, a movement cannot easily slow down of its own volition; it is too dependent on a mood of militancy. Followers fall away while leaders become confused by the need to press a rhetoric that ceases to conform to the realities. After Birmingham, as King was beginning to teach his followers to wait, he wrote a book entitled *Why We Can't Wait*. Since civil rights bills were before Congress, the movement could remain credible for a while longer, but it was in danger.

Out of these tensions came the extraordinary March on Washington of August 28, 1963, the symbolic culmination of the freedom marches, and the model for many demonstrations in other causes during the succeeding years. This strategically brilliant and psychologically perfect event exactly suited the needs of the situation. The idea had been that of Bayard Rustin, long an important radical activist for civil rights and socialism; the call came from A. Philip Randolph, dean of black labor leaders and originator of the March on Washington movement of 1941, which had persuaded Franklin Roosevelt to issue an order banning discrimination in war industries. But the march, originally designed to press for federal action on jobs, was quickly transformed by moderate white leaders, especially the clergy, into a demonstration in support of the civil rights bill pending in Congress. White liberals were in control; radical proposals by the more militant actionists were softened. Several liberal congressmen and senators joined the march as did a few labor leaders, headed by Walter Reuther of the United Auto Workers. The AFL-CIO national council declined to endorse it; here was a hint that the estrangement between labor and the civil rights movement, which had revealed itself in the early sixties, was becoming a serious split. Promoted by liberals, who insisted on limits to the tactics of the marchers—keeping them from Capitol Hill, discouraging acts of civil disobedience, and toning down the most radical speakers—the march received presidential endorsement.

The demonstration was a precious moment in American history. The gentle army of over two hundred thousand, mostly black but with many whites, assembled under Daniel Chester French's great statue of Lincoln to hear a medley of speeches and performers that caught the moods of the day and the moral direction of the times. Randolph saw the realization of a hope over twenty years old. Roy Wilkins eulogized W. E. B. DuBois, who as much as any other individual had created the forces in triumph on that August day—and who, by some miracle of historical fitness, had died the night before at the age of 95, disillusioned, expatriated, and totally alienated from the nation that only now was showing its willingness to meet the challenge he had posed. Martin Luther King articulated the dream of black history: the dream that came to Frederick Douglass and DuBois and Booker T. Washington of black men in America "Free at last." But a speech by John Lewis, SNCC chairman, which he had tempered when white religious leaders threatened not to attend if he spoke according to his original intentions, still unmistakably suggested that a revolutionary change in American institutions would be necessary before blacks could achieve equality. The march was indeed, as the President noted, something of which "the nation [could] properly be proud."

The "movement" phase of the revolution did not end at the Lincoln Memorial on that August Wednesday. The moral authority of the leaders had been based on the courage of the demonstrators, and men like King had gone to jail many times. Even the NAACP had committed itself to direct action at its 1963 convention. But the main attention had clearly passed to legislative and political activity: lobbying for the civil rights bills, registering voters, and trying to thwart the white backlash that emerged in municipal elections in Philadelphia and Chicago that year, and that the leaders rightly feared had a long future. This unquestionably meant holding demonstrations to a minimum and keeping down the more extreme forms of protest. Liberal allies such as the President and the liberal newspapers vigorously supported the leadership in these endeavors. Men like King found themselves caught between the dynamics of their organizations and the needs of the national movement for moderation and patience.

The radicals responded in most cases with even more confusion. The new demands brought great internal conflict in groups, such as SNCC and CORE, that had been both radical and a part of the cooperative strategy. The millennial impulse had little place to turn but inward in many cases, to a radical assessment of motivations and a painful testing of allies. The instabilities of the union between white and black youths emerged under the strategy of cooperation with dominant liberal institutions. The black youths had stressed their militancy, young whites their lack of racism and their radicalism. The rhetorical emphasis on black militancy increased as outlets were denied or became less satisfactory; the white civil rights workers could now find within the movement tests of their freedom from racism. The white workers were on the average far better trained to do the tasks of negotiating and administration, and their expertise had often given them special positions within the movement; black radicals therefore turned upon the predominantly white infrastructure, and their white allies had to accept, with whatever bitterness, the logic of the attack. The psychology of both groups called for the Negroes to drive out the whites. The white activists ended in the same position as the client-centered liberals with whom events had yoked them: suffering an ingratitude that had to be accepted because it was an indication of the health and progress they had originally sought for their clients.

While some radicals of both races retreated into a wasting

spiritual and psychological crisis, others were turning to the intricacies of American political institutions. The voter registration drive, which could be among the most daring possible acts in some places, took much energy. The trial of its import for the radicals came in 1964 with the Mississippi Freedom Democratic Party. At the Democratic Convention of 1964 this SNCC-sponsored group, a product of heroic voter registration work that cost several lives, challenged the credentials of the regular delegation from Mississippi. The ultimate issue would be the sincerity of the Democratic party; in its interests the major party spokesmen were urging a cool summer in the ghettos.

Party leaders showed how far they would go by offering to seat a portion of the Freedom Democratic delegation and by pledging that they would exact racial standards from all delegations at the next convention. Important figures such as King urged the young radicals to accept the proposal. They refused, retaining the independence of their party rather than entering into the normal process of political compromises. The tiny party, which two years later metamorphosed into the Black Panthers, was to have a phoenixlike existence in the netherworld of the urban ghettos, far from its origins in Mississippi. After the 1964 convention, groups like SNCC and then the Black Panthers took on the mystique of black nationalism; a few people, principally Martin Luther King, searched for a course that would work through piecemeal gains to the millennial dream they had glimpsed in the early sixties. The mid-sixties was a time of accomplishment in civil rights, a harvest season of the earlier planting, but the civil rights movement that had given the decade its flavor—flamed its radicalisms and made its liberalism meaningful— was dead, a sacrificial offering for the achievements and an atonement for the failures of the decade.

the johnson coalition

Chapter Five   Lyndon Johnson will be remembered as one of the great Chief Executives. He initiated more major laws for racial justice, education, health, the arts, the cities, and the ending of poverty than any earlier occupant of the White House. Ralph Ellison, the black novelist, said of Johnson as late as 1967 that he would perhaps "have to settle for being recognized as the greatest American President for the poor and for the Negroes, but that, as I see it, is a very great honor indeed."

    Yet it was the fate of Johnson to bring to fulfillment those liberal impulses in recent American life that, at their fulfillment, achieved their own contradiction and rout. A poverty program that went to the limits of political possibility in America became an object of contempt for white and ghetto radicals who had learned to think beyond the technocratic institutions of the liberal welfare state; and it provided, in its community action projects, an unwitting means to the organization of the young and the discontented into militant political undergrounds. The policy of containment that had been given its sharpest presidential statement during the Kennedy years, and in the test ban treaty had been well on the way to self-liquidation, resulted in a war it could neither avoid within its own assumptions nor satisfactorily wage, having denied to itself an apocalyptic rhetoric of vindication.

Lyndon Johnson was a proud, daring, and very political man. His strength, and his weakness, lay in a naive faith that in America government could accomplish all things. His confidence came of the New Deal and was embodied in the heroic figure of Franklin Roosevelt. Raised in an impoverished section of Texas, Johnson earned his way through a state college and gained experience teaching children of varied ancestry in a small country school. Phenomenally ambitious, he went to Washington in 1931 as secretary to a conservative congressman, and soon took politics for his natural habitat. After serving a term heading the National Youth Administration in Texas, Johnson successfully ran for Congress in 1937, basing his campaign on his loyalty to Franklin Roosevelt. The President returned the compliment and tried to get Johnson into the Senate. When Roosevelt died in 1945 the Washington editor of the *New York Times* chose Johnson to interview as a typical Democratic congressman bereft of his leader. Lyndon Johnson's first strong political identification, then, was with the New Deal and its advanced social programs.

Johnson had an instinct for power and knew how to get it. When Texas politics went conservative after World War II, Johnson shaped new alliances with the burgeoning aircraft industry and eventually won over most of the great powers of oil and natural gas. In the Eightieth Congress he joined in overriding President Truman's veto of the Taft-Hartley Act, which limited the privileges of labor. Johnson was finally elected to the Senate in 1948 and became an apprentice to Georgia's conservative Senator Richard Russell, who could grant important committee posts to aspiring protégés. Russell, and later the powerful Senator Robert Kerr of Oklahoma, came to admire Johnson for his energetic devotion to his job and forgave him his solitary position outside the solid Southern Caucus. Such a man as Johnson, supremely confident, evidently conservative yet able to communicate with northern liberals like Senator Hubert Humphrey of Minnesota, could be useful to the segregationist bloc.

Johnson's career had reached its least constructive point in the late forties and early fifties, when he complained about the intrusion of the race issue into the Senate's legislative affairs. When in 1950 he directed a Senate Commerce Subcommittee investigation of Leland Olds, a member of the Federal Power Commission and strong advocate of government regulation of the oil and gas interests, his treatment of Olds included highly illiberal tactics. Yet as leader of his party in the Senate, which he became in 1953, Johnson turned out to be a champion of moderation in domestic affairs and of a bipartisan foreign policy. He worked to hold together northern liberals and southern conservatives; and the practical Texan supported President Eisenhower as often as he could, saving his attacks for more vulnerable Republicans.

On some issues, Johnson wielded his powerful Senate leadership in the cause of conservatism. He was in an economy mood, scrapping with liberal senators on the matter of public spending, and his killing of the 1956 civil rights bill and weakening of the one passed in 1957 sent them into rebellion. But his policies were fairly bland and changeable. As soon as sputnik began to circle the night skies and the economy entered its third recessionary period in the decade, he abandoned his calls for thrift and pushed for public works, more unemployment compensation, and higher defense spending. In an effort to avoid presidential vetoes he would sometimes trim spending bills, but he had reversed himself on the issue of economy in government. In 1959 he pleased liberals by aiding in the defeat of Eisenhower's conservative nominee to be Secretary of Commerce, Admiral Lewis Strauss. In 1960 he joined the race for the Democratic presidential nomination, but though he entered no primaries it quickly became evident that his southern origins precluded his winning; Kennedy's Catholicism had compensating advantages that Johnson's regional background lacked. He settled for the second place.

Lyndon Johnson found his new executive office an isolated spot compared with the Senate leadership. Little power gravitated to him in the new administration. Kennedy gave him primary control over Texas patronage and appointed him head of the President's Committee on Equal Employment. Here he did a creditable job; he excelled at speaking sincerely and courageously for civil rights, notably in speeches at Gettysburg and Detroit—and in a southern accent. Johnson, however, wanted to be far more active and tried to maneuver into public view as a leader in the space race. He even upstaged John Kennedy before photographers by holding a telephone receiver simulating communication with the first American astronaut hurtling through space, while the President was shown facing his television set, a passive spectator.

Johnson as Vice-President took delight in traveling about the world as an emissary of the United States. He performed best in Berlin on a weekend in 1961, reassuring the citizenry in face of the oppressive wall being raised up by the Communists. Johnson had always been a hard-liner on the Cold War: in the fifties he had contemptuously rejected the conciliatory Stevensonian approach toward communism, declaring in 1954 that Red China should never be admitted to the United Nations and helping Hubert Humphrey in that year to pass a bill outlawing the American Communist party; and his vice-presidential rhetoric was martial. After a famous meeting in 1961 with Premier Diem of South Vietnam he waxed eloquent about the "Churchill of Asia" who would "fight communism in the streets and alleys, and when his hands are torn, he will fight it with his feet!"

Johnson behaved admirably before the public in the days right after the Kennedy assassination. He did everything he could to reassure the nation that Kennedy's memory would be served, and he appointed a distinguished panel under Chief Justice Earl Warren to investigate the killing. Kennedy's advisers were all persuaded to stay on, at least for a time. Johnson's administrations, in fact, were in basic continuity with Kennedy's. Both men used essentially the same corps of foreign policy advisers. In Vietnam Kennedy might easily have followed a course similar to Johnson's, believing that a limited war would inevitably be a prudent and tempered affair rather than the reckless undertaking it was to become. Had he lived, Kennedy might have expanded his social programs into something like the Great Society of his successor; just before his death his advisers were drafting proposals on poverty to present to Congress. And the sophistication that the Kennedy phenomenon brought to politics made it possible for Americans to think beyond the old shibboleths against "creeping socialism."

Perhaps it was the fact of the presidency itself, compelling Johnson, with his instinct for aggressive mastery, to seize upon some one powerful program for his leadership to achieve. That, and growth, and conscience. Whatever the reasons, the politician whose commitments had been almost undiscoverable through the shifts of three decades came to a complete and articulate unity. He gathered into a policy of reform at home and consolidation abroad much of what had existed for several years merely as trend or latency; and he completed and presided over a liberal coalition that had been some years in forming. The loose coalition is a typical phenomenon of American politics, a way of united political action for a people too diverse to organize along the lines of class, and disinclined to sharp political ideology. Such coalitions as Johnson's are familiar historical events, accomplishing the work of a generation in a brief surge of activity, as in the Wilsonian phase of the Progressive Movement (1913–1916), or the early New Deal (1933–1935). The Johnson, or Kennedy-Johnson, coalition enjoyed an active but ephemeral life for about three years, beginning in the spring of 1963. It was a working alliance among groups some of which had little mutual affection: civil rights forces; the poor, white as well as black; moderate southerners; organized labor, too strongly attracted by the spending policies of the new economics and too loyal to the Democratic party to break with the administration over the issue of race; and parts of the middle class pleased at economic conditions and seeking an improvement in government services. Citizens liberal by conviction supported the Kennedy-Johnson policies for their domestic programs and, until 1965, for their espousal of a temperate foreign policy untainted by the chauvinist anticommunism of the right. The most important addition to the coalition's strength came from many businessmen, who, as Robert Lekachman has noted, set the limits of its programs. In this the liberal coalition of the 1960s followed its predecessors; they, too, had flourished in periods of cooperation between business and liberal forces. The life of the coalition depended on prosperity, the confining of the civil rights movement by and large to the South, and the absurdity—or at least prematurity—of the Goldwater opposition in 1964.

The legislative logjam of 1963 began to crack even before Kennedy's assassination, and the tax bill of February 1964 was distinctly a Kennedy achievement. In less than six years the Senate had reversed its views on the efficacy of a tax cut as a means to quicken an ailing economy. When Senator Douglas had asked for a $6 billion tax cut in 1958 he was rebuffed by a vote of 65 to 23. Yet in February 1964, 76 senators favored a tax cut of over $10 billion—and at a time when the economy was merely lagging. By 1965 the new rates had stimulated production and reduced unemployment to the lowest level in eight years. As the conservative economic adviser to Goldwater, Milton Friedman, later announced: "Now we are all Keynesians." The government was actually collecting more revenue under the lower tax schedule that it had a year before under a higher one.

On civil rights, the preeminent issue of the era, President Kennedy had made a slow start, and even the bill he sent to Congress in June 1963 provided for only partial desegregating of public accommodations. There was still the fear on Kennedy's part that the stronger his position on civil rights the less he would accomplish elsewhere. But even before his death it had become apparent that powerful forces were converging in favor of a meaningful civil rights act. Peaceful demonstrations, as well as violence in Birmingham during May 1963, had an indirect effect on federal legislators by forcing some exemplary laws through on the local and state level. Then for the first time the nation's churches—so effective in promoting the prohibition movement more than a generation earlier—entered the civil rights movement in force. They would have a special influence in the Senate, which held the threat of a filibuster, for they could influence church-oriented members whose support was needed to shut off debate. Senator Everett Dirksen, minority leader and head of his party's uncommitted moderates, was besieged by churchmen, as well as by liberal Republicans and the new President who, a White House assistant remarked, "never let him alone for thirty minutes." The vote to end the southern filibuster in June 1964, taken after ample time had been allowed for a full expression of views, was 71 to 29, and then the bill itself passed by a slightly greater margin. The minority tallies included only five Republicans from outside the South, notably Barry Goldwater, and even fewer nonsouthern Democrats. It was the first time the Senate had ever invoked cloture on civil rights. The bill outlawed racial discrimination in all public places and in federally aided programs, as well as by employers and unions. Enforcement provisions were stronger than any that had existed previously. Subsequently it became fashionable to employ blacks; banks, law firms, and industries concerned with their public image offered them managerial positions.

Remembering the New Deal, Johnson observed that "great social change tends to come rapidly in periods of intense activity before the impulse slows"; after the civil rights victory of 1964 he pushed ahead with other plans. He found politically irresistible the idea of a "war" on poverty to be undertaken before the election. Michael Harrington, author of *The Other America* (1962), and other publicists had written feelingly of human beings lost in self-perpetuating poverty in Appalachia, the migrant farms of California, Indian reservations, urban ghettos, and even in the midst of plenty—just hidden from public view. Here President Kennedy had made a good beginning; he had advanced programs that could converge into the war on poverty, including area redevelopment, retraining of the unemployed, accelerated public works, eradication of illiteracy, and youth employment. But these programs were uncoordinated and some, like urban renewal, only destroyed precious cultural neighborhoods or merely pushed the poor from one slum to another. Johnson himself was well suited to declare war on poverty; during his youth he had been acquainted with it at firsthand in the Texas hill country. The "war" was a radical concept; its novel community action agencies, of which Mobilization for Youth was the prototype, incidentally opened the way to establishing new power bases from which the poor might challenge the rusting political machines, both urban and rural, that no longer seemed to care about them. The Job Corps, emphasizing vocational training and remedial education in urban slums, was immediately successful, and Volunteers in Service to America (VISTA) stimulated some of the same young enthusiasm that Kennedy's Peace Corps had evoked. The poverty program appealed to altruistic liberals with its bold objective of wiping out poverty, and to conservatives by deemphasizing "relief" and accentuating opportunity. In the election year, when opposing the Economic Opportunity Act would be construed as favoring poverty, the near-billion-dollar appropriation easily passed Congress.

There the record stood when Congress recessed in preparation for the 1964 elections. That spring Walter Lippmann observed that "the country is far more united and at peace with itself, except over the issue of Negro rights, than it has been for a long time. [Johnson has] done, I think, what President Kennedy could not have done had he lived." Johnson, now of a great and expansive will, took advantage of the prevailing climate. One of his speech writers, Richard Goodwin, hit on the phrase "the Great Society," and Johnson would spend the 1964 presidential campaign outlining major social programs for the future.

The Democratic nominee in 1964 could only be Johnson, who wanted the Atlantic City convention to hold but one uncertainty: who would be the vice-presidential nominee. The President gave the drama of expectation a cruel flavor, dangling the prize before one prospective nominee and then another, playing out the performance to the last painful moment. In retrospect it seems apparent that he had only one candidate fixed in mind: Hubert Humphrey. Bobby Kennedy, whom Johnson disliked, had been put out of consideration for the vice-presidency in an edict that eliminated all of the cabinet on the grounds that they were needed to run the government. Another possible choice, Humphrey's Minnesota colleague in the Senate, Eugene McCarthy, was much too reserved and too independent for Johnson. Soon after the affable Humphrey had become a senator, Johnson had singled him out for special attention, and from time to time the Texan had managed to persuade the liberal Minnesotan, with his tendency toward moralistic brashness, to put his energies behind programs standing a chance of passage. At the 1964 convention the faithful Humphrey effected a compromise that forced most of the regular Mississippi delegation to go home rather than sign an oath of loyalty to the nominees, and left as representatives of the state a counterdelegation of blacks, equally dissatisfied because of the compromising on a moral issue, to represent the state.

In contrast to the well-organized Democrats, the Republicans were in disarray from the start. Governor Nelson Rockefeller of New York faced Senator Barry Goldwater of Arizona in the early New Hampshire primary, but neither man won. The victor in a walkaway was write-in candidate Henry Cabot Lodge, the liberal Republican ambassador to Vietnam hard at work some nine thousand miles away. It was held against Rockefeller that he had divorced his wife after twenty-four years of marriage, and in May 1963 had married again. Knowing that he guarded the more modern wing of the party against what he considered a dangerous right-wing threat, Rockefeller had behaved irresponsibly by his untimely personal demeanor. Goldwater, with such gestures as his offhand comment to New Hampshire voters about "defoliating" Vietnam with some atomic bombs, had almost resolutely achieved an image of imprudence. Rockefeller won the next important primary in Oregon, followed by Lodge and then Goldwater. The only primary Goldwater won, and that by a shade, came in California the weekend after the second Mrs. Rockefeller gave birth to a son and former President Eisenhower retracted an implicitly anti-Goldwater remark he had made.

Goldwater's strength in the states where no primaries were held was so solid, however, that a single major primary victory was sufficient. Liberal Republican opposition by Governors William Scranton of Pennsylvania and George Romney of Michigan came too late. Goldwater's nomination on the first ballot in the San Francisco convention is a testament to the effectiveness of a determined minority, the cadres of right-wing true believers who had seized control of local Republican organizations. Possibly, of course, some Republican leaders looked on Goldwater as a calculated risk. In a year so bleak, they might as well test the proposition on which the right wing had long insisted, that a politically fundamentalist America untouched by recent candidacies would waken at the proper voice. "Anyone who joins us in all sincerity we welcome," Barry Goldwater announced in his acceptance speech. "Those who do not care for our cause, we don't expect to enter our ranks." He chose Representative William Miller, an upstate New York reactionary, as his running mate. The Roman Catholic Miller, some said, offered only a photogenic family and a vitriolic tongue.

The vagaries of the Goldwater campaign were remarkable. Relations with moderate Republicans worsened. Such figures as Romney of Michigan and Rockefeller of New York remained determinedly aloof from the Goldwater effort. The candidate himself backed off from some earlier ghostwritten statements in his *The Conscience of a Conservative* and *Why Not Victory?* But in Appalachia he denounced the poverty program as cynical, phony, and irresponsible —and called on free enterprise to defeat poverty. In Knoxville, Tennessee, he stuck by his position in favor of selling parts of the government-owned Tennessee Valley Authority; in St. Petersburg, Florida, he criticized Social Security enough to make old people fear he really did favor its abolition, as Democrats charged. He told North Dakota farmers he thought a gradual decline in price supports would be good for them. In South Bend, Indiana, on Labor Day, vice-presidential candidate Miller scored liberalized immigration policies before an audience composed chiefly of first- and second-generation Americans. Such naive "honesty" presented the Democrats with an embarrassment of riches. One television commercial showed a Social Security card being ripped in two. Another one was particularly objectionable: it had a little girl plucking petals from a daisy; in the background a voice intoned the countdown for an atomic test, and when the picture dissolved into a mushroom cloud, the voice said: "Vote for President Johnson on November 3. The stakes are too high for you to stay at home."

Through such devices the Democrats succeeded in portraying the doctrinaire and impolitic Goldwater as a reckless man who could not be trusted with the button that could signal nuclear war. In August when Goldwater spoke against the administration's "no-win" foreign policy, making it appear that he would commit some grand act of military glory against international communism, Johnson executed a limited retaliatory bombing in response to what was alleged to be a North Vietnamese attack on an American ship. At the same time Johnson worked at picturing himself as a temperate man who could be trusted with atomic weapons, a builder interested in policies and programs. The President, Richard Rovere noted, "moved from a defense of past Democratic administrations to evangelistic and almost utopian views of the future." Yet his program, however bold its sweep, was in the tradition of the New Deal. The welfare state Johnson and Humphrey represented had become so much a part of America that many regular Republicans sensed the essentially radical character of the Goldwater forces. What man of conservative instinct would risk replacing Social Security and crop subsidies with some ill-defined adventure against global communism? In the entire campaign only two incidents momentarily threatened Johnson's confidence. The first, a New York City race riot in the summer, came just after the Republican National Convention adjourned. But voters apparently perceived that a law and order candidate such as Goldwater promised greater social conflict rather than less. On October 15 it was revealed that a close assistant to Johnson had been arrested after police caught him in a homosexual act, but he was a likable man, a hard worker and good husband; and in face of the revelation the public showed a maturity observers would not have dared predict. Besides, there was a cliff-hanging World Series; and then the next day Nikita Khrushchev was deposed in Russia, and a day later the Communist Chinese exploded their first atom bomb.

Born to be exploited by a capable politician like Lyndon Johnson, Goldwater lost the election by an overwhelming margin in the popular vote, 43,000,000 to 27,000,000. He carried only his home state, along with Georgia, South Carolina, Alabama, Louisiana, and Mississippi (where he received 87 percent of the vote) for a total of 52 electoral votes against Johnson's 486. The President's 61.1 percent of the two-party vote was a record. Such were the fruits of Goldwater's all-out use of a "southern strategy," although its employment was to some extent simply premature. The race issue was not yet ripe: the civil rights movement was largely confined to the South until 1965, and there under the leadership of Martin Luther King it generally managed to avoid too violent a posture. In the Senate the Democrats maintained their 2-to-1 majority, and an increase of 38 Democrats in the House—giving them a margin of 295 to 140—ensured that Johnson's Great Society programs would coast through the new Congress.

Whether the defeat of Barry Goldwater indicated that right-wing attitudes had little appeal in America is not quite clear. The racist candidate, George Wallace, had run very well in some early Democratic primaries before he dropped out of the campaign in favor of Goldwater. Perhaps the presidential election is too inclusive and murky on issues to provide such a test. The Goldwater candidacy marshaled opposition to "liberalism" that could yet have a substantial impact in the years ahead. On the other hand, the lopsided margin of defeat guaranteed that no extreme conservative would soon be nominated again by the Republican party, as the defeat of Al Smith had contributed to preventing the Democrats even from considering the possibility of another Roman Catholic for a generation.

What followed the 1964 election was a brilliant manipulation of Congress by President Johnson, who continued to capitalize on the memory of Kennedy as well as on his own longstanding legislative skills. A survivor of the New Deal, Johnson knew that the liberal coalition he had constructed might have a short life. Nineteen-sixty-five was an *annus mirabilis* for the passage of liberal legislation.

Comprehensive and massive aid to primary and secondary education had floundered in Congress for a decade, for it was related to two particularly controversial issues: race and relations between church and state. In President Eisenhower's second term, Congressman Adam Clayton Powell of Harlem attached an antisegregation amendment to a good education bill, driving into opposition some southerners who were among the strongest supporters of aid to education, and the amended bill lost. Then in 1961 Catholic congressmen refused to support a measure omitting substantial support for parochial schools, while Protestant churchmen, aided by the public school lobby, objected to such support in principle. Although piecemeal victories were won between 1958 and 1964, it was 1965 before large-scale support for elementary and secondary schools won passage.

No one wanted a religious squabble in 1965 while the memory of John Kennedy remained fresh. In that year President Johnson proposed a measure aiding special programs in parochial schools to avoid a Catholic veto, but not enough to risk loss of the public school lobby. New civil rights acts had removed the necessity of tying antisegregation amendments to education aid. The House passed the billion-dollar education measure by a vote of 263 to 153, and only 18 senators voted nay. To sign the bill into law, Johnson flew to the rural schoolhouse in Texas where he had once taught.

The last major legislative foundation in the Great Society was Medicare, health care for the aged funded through Social Security. Back in the 1930s and 1940s the problem of medical aid for people over sixty-five had been subsumed within the larger issue of assured treatment for the entire population. But when the American Medical Association denounced President Truman's plan for universal health insurance as socialized medicine and launched against it the most lavish lobbying campaign in American history, the doctors forced the liberals into retreat, and they worked to achieve the more modest and compelling ambition of care for the aged. During the 1950s both Democrats and Republicans proposed private health insurance schemes for the elderly. The labor movement, however, set Congress on the track of a broad program to provide health care for the elderly under Social Security. And by 1960 the medical profession no longer stood as an unbroken phalanx in opposition to Social Security financing. A Medicare bill advanced by John Kennedy in 1960 fell victim to politics in the summer before the presidential campaign, when even liberal Republicans would not support it, and the new Congress was too conservative to pass the measure. It took the 1964 Democratic landslide to settle the question of Medicare. The law, which passed the Senate in 1965 by a vote of 68 to 21, contained a deductible item and a maximum limit on coverage, but it was a giant advance. Furthermore, it included a little-known section called Medicaid that provided medical care to families earning less than a minimum figure.

Other laws passed quickly in these years: aid for mass transit in 1964; and in 1965 another major antipoverty program, rent supplements for lower-income families, and funds for model cities, housing, public works, and regional health centers, where research and treatment of heart disease and cancer would be coordinated.

On these Great Society programs criticism on the part of business was muted or nonexistent. During the 1950s, by contrast, Eisenhower's more liberal cabinet members had been discouraged by massive business opposition from spending in the public sector of the economy. But in the Kennedy period businessmen began to have second thoughts. The great era of capital investment that began in the early sixties required a larger labor supply, and so business supported a liberal reform of immigration laws under Kennedy. It also became interested in the various programs by which Kennedy was trying to curb unemployment. If job training meant supplying labor in important fields where labor was scarce, it was of obvious benefit to the large corporations. And in Johnson's poverty program big businesses even lent their personnel to training centers to expedite the process of what amounted to another subsidy for business. Finally, business had an interest in a social calm that the welfare measures of the Great Society might maintain.

The Great Society's notable failure came in an area that would become major by the end of the decade, that of ecology. As late as 1960, President Eisenhower had referred to water pollution as "a uniquely local blight." "Primary responsibility for solving the problem," he said in a message vetoing a pollution control bill, "lies not with the Federal Government but rather . . . [with] . . . State and local governments." Industry agreed with the President. Kennedy, too, moved slowly on environmental matters and gave slight support to Senator Edmund Muskie's bill of 1963 transferring water pollution control from the slow-moving Public Health Service to a new agency in the Department of Health, Education, and Welfare. Not until September 1964 did the House Public Works Committee report such a bill, which ten of the fourteen Republicans criticized as "premature, unnecessary, and undesirable."

Again, real progress awaited the Johnson coalition. The Water Quality Act of 1965, which passed the Senate by a vote of 90 to 0, authorized a $6 billion expenditure. And in 1966 the Clean Water Restoration Act removed the ceiling from individual grants under the program. But in 1968 less than half of the $450 million appropriation was spent, and the following year less than one-third of $700 million. Such was the course of many Great Society programs—large appropriations from Congress but executive restraint in spending—once the costly Vietnam war was in full flame.

Air pollution, a more immediate threat to health than bad water, is caused in great part by automotive exhaust fumes. General Motors,

Ford, and Chrysler had been putting styling ahead of safety considerations and had ignored the problem of pollution. When Ralph Nader published *Unsafe at Any Speed* (1965), a book that exposed the industry's blatant disregard of safety standards, General Motors shocked the informed public by hiring an investigating firm to probe for something compromising in the young lawyer's private life. Senator Muskie again took a position of leadership by introducing legislation to prescribe standards of exhaust emission for gasoline-powered vehicles. Johnson, whose Great Society intended business as one of its active components, stalled on the touchy question of putting a 1967 deadline in Muskie's bill. When the bill was finally passed, the enforcement date was left to administrative discretion.

By 1966 the Johnson coalition was in process of breaking up. The first specific issue to threaten it was, of course, that of civil rights and civil disorder. Johnson was obliged to ask for passage of the 1964 Civil Rights Act; he could not simply assume any of the Democratic coalition's northern constituency—and especially the Negro, who might be pushed beyond the point of coalition politics. But the sincerity of his devotion to the cause became clear in the next two years. Johnson was willing to risk loss of ethnic support; the long-promised "backlash" of the white working class, resentful of special treatment for blacks, was beginning to materialize. In 1965 he asked the Justice Department what else could be done before the reform impulse weakened. The department suggested that voting rights needed strengthening. An occasion to press for new legislation came in the spring of 1965 when Negro freedom marchers were repelled at Selma, Alabama, by police using clubs, whips, and ropes. Speaking in person before both Houses of Congress, the President presented a new tactic for voter registration in seven southern states, and the result was the Civil Rights Act of 1965. According to the new law, most voter registration would be accomplished henceforth not by "tedious" lawsuits but immediately by federal examiners.

In January 1966 Johnson offered still another major civil rights request in his State of the Union message. He took a radical step by recommending laws prohibiting discrimination in the sale or rental of all housing. Johnson also asked that a federal crime be made of interference with the rights of others in voting, education, housing, employment, jury service, and travel. Both bills passed, but the weakened housing measure ran against emotions in the North. Before and after the bill was passed, realtors and homeowners deluged Congress and the President with protest. When Martin Luther King led a group of blacks into a white residential area in Chicago, the act enraged a white mob. "I have never seen such hatred—not in Mississippi or Alabama," said King. By 1966 the Negro was no longer pictured in the public mind as a praying, nonviolent victim of southern "justice"; three summers of urban riots had discharged that image, replacing it with that of black power and the Molotov cocktail. The law and order issue unquestionably contributed to the Republican victories in the congressional elections, where that party gained 47 seats in the House and 4 in the Senate.

Those off-term congressional elections came too early for a registration of sentiment against the Vietnam war. We had joined in full force some twenty months before, and President Johnson's advisers were promising an early victory. It gradually became evident, however, that the social conflicts of the later sixties would be orchestrated around the overwhelming fact of our involvement in Vietnam. In 1966 the Johnson legislative program was largely completed and the war reached full fury.

The small country of Vietnam, almost halfway around the world from us, had fallen under French control in the latter part of the nineteenth century. Well before World War II the French colonialists had been challenged by nationalist leaders such as Ho Chi Minh, who had become a Communist in Europe during the 1920s. During and after the war, with the distinct encouragement of Harry Truman and his Secretary of State Dean Acheson, the French attempted to regain control of Indochina through a puppet emperor and a façade of national independence. Ho took the leadership in evicting the colonialists and in doing so knit nationalism and communism together in Vietnam as in no other Southeast Asian country. The French fought a valiant but hopeless European-style war in the jungles of Vietnam; during the siege at Dien Bien Phu in 1954, a year after the signing of the Korean armistice, their commander pleaded for American support—perhaps even an air strike with atomic weapons. Admiral Radford, chairman of the Joint Chiefs of Staff, and Vice-President Nixon advocated sending American troops to Vietnam, while Secretary of State Dulles recommended some kind of air strike. But contrary advice prevailed. Army Chief of Staff Matthew Ridgway declared flatly against intervention. Secretary of Defense Charles Wilson and Secretary of the Treasury George Humphrey counseled against it. Lyndon Johnson, then minority leader in the Senate, also opposed involvement in the absence of allied support, and Britain refused to back an American commitment. President Eisenhower, a man of enormous military prestige, decided against unilateral intervention, saying he "could conceive of no greater tragedy than for the United States to become involved in an all-out war in Vietnam."

The French phase of hostilities came to an end at the Geneva Conference of 1954. The agreements provided for a temporary division of Vietnam at the seventeenth parallel and free elections to be held throughout the country within two years. Nationwide elections, however, were never held. Ngo Dinh Diem, another early nationalist leader acting with American encouragement, took dictatorial command in the south and substituted his own rigged elections. Under Diem's leadership and with generous American support, some economic growth and even land reform materialized between about 1954 and 1957, but Diem failed to develop a base of popular support, and after his first years in power adopted increasingly repressive tactics. By the end of the decade the Vietcong, an indigenous revolutionary group not initially supported by North Vietnam, controlled much of the countryside.

It can be argued that the rhetoric of such a Cold War advocate as Dulles, the signing in 1954 of the Southeast Asia Collective Defense Treaty requiring "consultation" in case of regional disturbances, and a letter pledging conditional economic and political support that Eisenhower sent to Diem in 1955 established a kind of moral commitment. Certainly the Eisenhower policy had by 1961 created some sort of national interest in South Vietnam. Those favoring American intervention could then argue that neighboring governments had staked their own security on our ability to maintain stable rule there. If South Vietnam fell victim to communism, neighboring countries would soon discover a similar fate. Modeled on the analogy of Munich, where Britain and France sought to appease Hitler by giving up Czechoslovakia, this "domino" theory substituted communism for fascism and Asia for Europe.

Many critics place the largest share of blame on the Kennedy administration. The young President, they argue, was still carried along by the shock wave resulting from the Communist victory in China and the French collapse in Vietnam. After the Vietcong force was strengthened by some 6000 southerners who had been trained in the North, Kennedy in 1961 faced a crisis that threatened Saigon itself. He decided to send thousands of American troops—more than 16,000 by 1963—including many Green Beret units, to Vietnam in part as a warning to the Russians. Only 900 such "advisers" had been there when Eisenhower left office. Prompted by a report by Walt Rostow and the new chairman of the Joint Chiefs of Staff, Maxwell Taylor, Kennedy also introduced artillery and fighter-bomber aircraft in South Vietnam. The result was a temporary setback for the Vietcong in 1962. Once the American presence had been established, however, it was unlikely that its size or character could be limited. When American troops are committed and some are killed, those who advocate escalation will employ the irresistible logic of redemption. Kennedy himself must have realized this, for he remarked that sending troops is a little like taking a drink: the effect wears off and you have to take another. Each new escalation was carried out with the obsessive certainty that it would ultimately succeed.

Kennedy's thoughts on Vietnam are difficult to decipher, and his defenders insist that he would have avoided a full-scale land war there. He certainly did have doubts. In September 1963 the President remarked: "In the final analysis it is their war," but he also said: "For the United States to withdraw . . . would mean a collapse not only of South Vietnam but Southeast Asia. So we are going to stay there." The August decision to curtail support for Diem, which led to his assassination late in October, provided an opportunity for a policy shift. *Time* suggested the possibility of neutralizing all of Southeast Asia, and in a National Security Council meeting Robert Kennedy asked whether it might be a good time to leave South Vietnam, but the President had advanced no plans along these lines by the time of his own death. Defenders of Kennedy insist that a limited effort to shore up Vietnam, such as the course the President adopted, was worthwhile; a total effort, however, was anathema to him, and he planned to withdraw after the 1964 elections. Yet the war in Vietnam, at least in its initial stages, was made for the kind of limited guerrilla fighting that Kennedy, his Secretary of Defense Robert McNamara, and General Maxwell Taylor had been anticipating. They wanted to demonstrate to the Russians, in Taylor's words, that wars of national liberation were not "cheap, safe, and disavowable" but "costly, dangerous, and doomed to failure." Whether the army itself had been made ready for such a war is questionable. What Taylor and Rusk and Rostow did not adequately appreciate, moreover, was that in all parts of the world something was going on that did not begin in Moscow, Peking, or Washington. It was a revolutionary condition born in the soil of each land it inhabited.

When Lyndon Johnson became President in 1963, he was caught in the momentum of past commitments by four American presidents. In 1964, acting with encouragement from virtually all of Kennedy's remaining military and foreign advisers, President Johnson set in motion a military escalation in Vietnam. During the campaign Johnson ordered a retaliatory air strike against North Vietnam after a second alleged shelling of an American ship in the Gulf of Tonkin. Johnson then requested and got an important Senate resolution that gave him a free hand in conducting the war. No doubt the senators preferred to be relieved of the painful decisions the President might have to make, although they had no idea that he would embark on a massive land war. Johnson was on the way toward becoming the most powerful President the country had ever seen. In February 1965 he gave the order for systematic bombing of North Vietnam; the air force foolishly began its flights while Soviet Premier Aleksei

Kosygin was visiting Hanoi. In response to the bombing, Russia stepped up its aid to North Vietnam, which in turn accelerated its infiltration into the South. The bombing stiffened North Vietnam's support for the war and did not cut down on infiltration or even seriously damage supply routes. Designed to interdict fleets of modern trucks and trains, the bombing strategy failed to affect bicycle traffic and men carrying supplies on their backs. Its sole claim to success was the tenuous one of improving morale in Saigon: its monetary cost was at least $20 million a day. In July 1965 Johnson decided on an even more massive intervention. As hundreds of thousands of American troops and billions of American dollars poured into Southeast Asia, the premise that this was primarily a Vietnamese war could no longer be sustained.

During the Vietnam escalation President Johnson also intervened in a civil war in the Dominican Republic. Here he was relying on Thomas Mann, Assistant Secretary of State for Inter-American Affairs, who had little use for the liberals who supported the Alliance for Progress. A leftist revolt to restore the non-Communist but ineffectual leader Juan Bosch—who had won some 60 percent of the vote in a national election of 1962 before an army coup d'état overthrew him—broke out in April 1965. Johnson rushed marines in to protect American citizens and incidentally to maintain the ruling military junta. The President's Vietnam critics said he was overreacting, using force where restraint was needed; they labeled the intervention a Vietnam in microcosm. But this was the intervention we got away with.

Our foreign policy has not been formulated by a few Dr. Strangeloves, crazed militarists hidden in subterranean chambers of the Pentagon. Vietnam is a tragedy in almost the literary sense of the word, for as Arthur Schlesinger, Jr., has shown, it grew in part from a decent and intelligent tradition of collective security and liberal evangelism—a tradition of men like Woodrow Wilson and Henry L. Stimson, who believed that world order required the punishment of aggression. Franklin Roosevelt enlarged upon the Wilsonian dream in World War II, putting the New Deal on a global basis. By the 1960s we had the Johnson "Earth Control Clinic," which instituted the decimating of South Vietnam even as it offered an Asian Development Bank to rebuild all of Southeast Asia. Those who bear direct responsibility for escalating the war sharply in 1965 were not in Barry Goldwater's camp. They were liberal intellectuals. Dean Rusk had been a Rhodes Scholar. Robert McNamara, when he taught at the Harvard Business School, was one of two faculty members to favor Franklin Roosevelt for reelection in 1940. McGeorge Bundy, a close presidential adviser before he left the White House full of doubts in 1966, had been Dean of the Harvard Faculty of Arts and Sciences. Walt Rostow, the most tenacious of the White House hawks, had been a professor of economic history at M.I.T. and an early supporter of Kennedy.

It does an intelligent man like Dean Rusk little credit to suppose he was responding only to aggression from North Vietnam, which in numbers amounted to very little before our massive entry of 1965, or protecting, in South Vietnam, a freedom that did not flourish either there or in the North. Rather, the reason for our involvement was the encompassing architectural vision that guided the Cold War policy of containment. For even though that policy, in the very complexity of its effort, had increasingly taught us to particularize our planet into its separate economies and technologies, its specific nationalisms and revolutions, it had held to the notion that the world is roughly divisible into large configurations of power, and that aggression is not definable as a specific military excursion over a national boundary, but is a revolutionary coalition invisibly stretched from one land to another. If we had concerned ourselves with invasions as they are conventionally understood, we would have discovered the one in Southeast Asia to be nonexistent or too local to be our concern. But instead, we had the specter of Communist China. "It takes no vivid imagination," said William Bundy, Assistant Secretary for Far Eastern Affairs, in February 1966, "to visualize what Peking would do in Malaysia, Singapore, and Burma if Hanoi were to succeed in Vietnam . . ."; and our war aim in Southeast Asia was summed up very succinctly by Dean Rusk in March of that year: to ensure that China some day moves toward peaceful coexistence.

The American intervention in Vietnam, dictated by the greater architectonic conception of the Cold War, was a result also of a more specific technocratic belief: that in Southeast Asia we could computerize a victory. The Pentagon had it all rationally demonstrated —given so many enemy troops and cadres, concentrated so, they could be eliminated by such and such applications of firepower: and the electronic brain would tell where and how much. The confidence of the Pentagon reflected the narrow arrogance of the technician who wields machines and statistics, and the simplicity of men who believe in them.

Had the Vietnam war been swift and casualties light, the past assumptions of the Cold War would never have been questioned as they have. But the enemy met our every troop increase, and bombing his cities only firmed his resolve to fight. Whatever the moral shortcomings of the Vietcong in the eyes of the world, they seemed trifling compared to America's destruction of many more innocent people and much of the land with devastating firepower, our B-52s dropping on "suspect" villages cluster bombs maiming everyone within hundreds of feet, white phosphorus and unextinguishable napalm— jelled gasoline or "incinderjell" in the consumer-minded Pentagon, that fastens to human skin and inexorably burns into the body—and our support of a brutal and corrupt government. We destroyed many areas of the countryside with defoliants, forcing the people into urban slums where they could perhaps be controlled. And we did all this before newsmen and television cameras, in a war without organized censorship and with no consistent governmental will to mobilize public sentiment and deny dissent.

Even by the end of 1967 it was clear to many congressional leaders that we would not quickly win the war in Vietnam. The most powerful nation in the world could not soon defeat an army of peasants, operating without an air force, a navy, or heavy artillery, in a nation half the size of California, although the money we spent there could have paved the country with concrete. North Vietnam, by that year, was perhaps the most stable government in Southeast Asia. At home in America the war had broken the political and social consensus. By the end of March 1968, after the Tet offensive that almost destroyed the ancient city of Hue, and after Senator Eugene McCarthy ran well as a peace candidate in the New Hampshire primary, critics succeeded in toppling the Johnson government.

Mrs. Rosa Parks sits at the front of a city bus, December 1956, Mont-gomery, Alabama. (UPI)

Negroes stay unserved during lunch counter sit-down protest, 1960. Portsmouth, Virginia. (Jim Walker)

U.S. marshals and security agents escort James Meredith to classes at the University of Mississippi, 1962. (Pictorial Parade)

Civil rights protesters are arrested. Birmingham, Alabama, 1963. (Magnum)

Martin Luther King, Jr. (Wide World)

Police use fire hoses to disperse civil rights demonstrators, Birmingham, Alabama, 1963. (Pix, Inc.)

the march on washington, august 1963

The March on Washington, August 1963. "I Have a Dream" speech by
Martin Luther King. (Wide World)

Martin Luther King, Roy Wilkins, A. Philip Randolph, and others
lead march along Constitution Avenue. (UPI)

(Fred McDarrah)

Resurrection City, Washington, D.C., 1967. (Editorial Photocolor Archives)

Ku Klux Klan. (David Cupp)

Cassius Clay (now Muhammad Ali) in the ring. (David Cupp)

Representative Adam Clayton Powell, D.-N.Y. (Wide World)

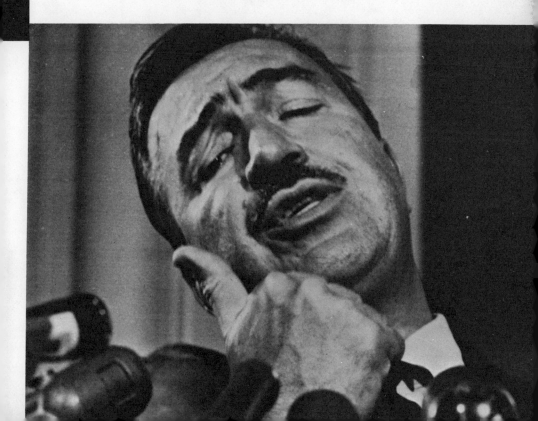

(George Gardner)

Black Studies. (Charles Gatewood)

Coretta King. (Wide World)

Martin Luther King funeral procession, Atlanta, 1968. (Wide World)

Washington, D.C., riots following the assassination of Martin Luther King, Jr., 1968. (Wide World)

(Richard Howard, Bethel)

Black Panthers protest at Criminal Courts Building to support 21 Panthers arrested in New York City, 1969. (Hap Stewart)

Black Panther protest for jailed Panthers awaiting trial, New York.
(Hap Stewart)

Julian Bond at Chicago Democratic Convention, 1968. (UPI)

1968-and after

Chapter Six At the end of January 1968, masses of Vietcong
soldiers simultaneously attacked every major city
in South Vietnam, and as government troops rushed
to defend the urban areas other VC expanded in
the countryside. The Tet offensive caught the Americans and their South Vietnamese allies by surprise;
the capital city of Saigon could have fallen to the
invaders, and large parts of many cities, notably
Hue in the north, were under enemy control for
days. The American Embassy itself came under
siege, and only the bloodiest counteroffensive
restored the cities to the Allies. The attacks had
taken on the character of nationalist uprisings. The
Vietcong had been organized with an absolute se-
crecy founded in discipline and dedication; they
stood in startling contrast to the venality and inef-
fectiveness of Premier Ky's ARVN forces.

In America, Tet followed an especially optimistic

army report of progress in South Vietnam. For years the Pentagon, the State Department, and the White House had been assuring the people that our position in Vietnam was improving and that an end to the war was in sight. Tet ripped at what remained of the Johnson coalition. When the facts filtered through to the public mind, the spectrum of dissent from the war widened considerably as important businessmen and isolationists joined radicals, liberals, and young people in opposing the war—although for differing motives and with differing alternative strategies in mind. After Tet no one fully trusted the administration's statements about Vietnam. President Johnson himself especially lost credibility. Only the most inveterate optimist now believed that victory, or even stalemate, could be reached without many years of fighting.

For some time the peace movement—initially a product of radical activists and pacifists—had lacked a prominent leader, although it was served faithfully in Congress by such senators as William Fulbright, Wayne Morse, George McGovern, and Ernest Gruening. Antiwar activities were organized on a national basis chiefly by Allard Lowenstein, a vigorous New York lawyer who had been approaching national politicians about leading the cause. Senator Robert Kennedy of New York, in many ways the most logical figure, was interested, but he misjudged the depth of antiwar sentiment and disliked radicals who carried Vietcong flags and marched on the Pentagon. He was also afraid that heading an abortive movement might leave him without support in future liberal causes. It turned out that he waited too long.

During the summer of 1967 Senator Eugene McCarthy of Minnesota, a handsome, gray-haired man of fifty-one, generally unruffled by events in the world at large, lost his composure during a hearing of the Senate Foreign Relations Committee. Attorney General Nicholas Katzenbach was explaining his views of presidential power in foreign affairs: things happened too fast nowadays, Katzenbach said, for a President to be able to consult the Senate before starting a war. McCarthy angrily objected that such extensive presidential authority left the Senate and the people at the mercy of the President.

McCarthy decided in late November 1967 to run in the forthcoming Democratic primaries, challenging the administration for "continued escalation and intensification of the war in Vietnam." The first test came in New Hampshire on March 12, long before the snow and frozen ground would give way to spring. A corps of warmly enthusiastic young people, led by some knowledgeable graduate students, carried the McCarthy message throughout the state. They were fortunate to have as adversaries a Democratic governor and senator whose heavy-handed patriotism alienated the independent New

Hampshire voters. The students were even more fortunate to have Eugene McCarthy, a man so dry and self-contained—almost a New Englander himself: he would make, he claimed, an "adequate" President. He refrained from insisting on the immorality and brutality of the war, emphasizing instead its cost in lives and money. He stood for cleansing and restoring old institutions, for an end to violence and discontent. McCarthy's campaign was more of an asset than many of his aggressive supporters realized; it won him admirers even among the vast number of Americans for whom students are unspeakable—and interview data show that many people unsympathetic to his basic position nevertheless supported him. Also, McCarthy is a Roman Catholic, as were 65 percent of the state's Democratic voters. The senator won 42 percent of the two-party vote, almost as much as Johnson's write-in total of 49 percent. It was unprecedented to run against an American war while the war was on, and to come within a few thousand votes of winning against an incumbent President.

McCarthy's strong showing made antiwar dissent respectable. Three days later Robert Kennedy announced that he too would oppose the President in primaries. Kennedy, who had won a New York Senate seat in 1966, had been maturing rapidly in the years since his brother's death. By 1968 he had come to a position that was both skeptical in expectation and wide in its commitments to domestic issues and especially to that of minorities. He wanted the war at an end so that the nation's resources could be directed toward solving its own problems; and he admitted to a share of guilt in the series of events leading to our involvement in Vietnam. That the announcement of his candidacy came only after McCarthy's startling victory suggested the bluntest kind of opportunism, though he had evidently decided to run some weeks before. But it showed his political pragmatism. Only a Kennedy, so he believed, could defeat Johnson: McCarthy could not, for he lacked a broad politics that appealed alike to blacks and many city bosses, to middle-class liberals and students.

Perhaps Kennedy's decision to run played an important part in the composition of a televised speech Lyndon Johnson delivered on March 31, just two days before the Wisconsin primary. The President dramatically announced that he had decided the time had come to deescalate the Vietnam war. He would cut back the bombing of North Vietnam and he was rejecting army pleas for more troops. Then in a surprise coda he remarked that since he wanted to devote full time to the search for peace, he would not seek reelection in November. The political field was now free to McCarthy, Kennedy, and Vice-President Humphrey. Johnson's withdrawal was a triumph for the peace forces, but it also presented problems for their candidates, now deprived of an easy enemy.

The rivalry between Kennedy and McCarthy became a highly personal one, fragmenting the peace movement. Kennedy thought McCarthy indolent, snobbish, and ineffectual; McCarthy, who had strongly opposed John Kennedy's nomination in 1960, disdained a streak of demagoguery and a dominant opportunism in Bobby. The two fought in primaries across the country and competed for the support of young people. McCarthy, after winning decisively against Johnson in Wisconsin, clearly lost in Indiana and Nebraska, then made a good rebound in Oregon. In what Kennedy had hoped would be their final contest, after which the loser would drop out, he rather narrowly defeated McCarthy in California on June 4. On the very night of the election Kennedy was shot dead by a Jordanian immigrant, Sirhan Bishara Sirhan. Only weeks before, on April 24, Martin Luther King, Jr., had fallen victim to a bullet fired by a racist, and riots followed in Washington, D.C., Baltimore, and other major cities.

Before Robert Kennedy died, Gene McCarthy had made a brilliant speech in San Francisco against the Vietnam war, finding the seeds of it in our past, when we had taken on the role of the world's judge. After the California primary, though, he made no attempt to mobilize the antiwar forces. In mid-June he ran very well in the New York primary. But he spent considerable time each day writing poetry and, as though pessimistic about the affairs of this world, withdrew for a while to a Benedictine retreat during the hectic weeks before the Democratic Convention met in Chicago; when popular polls failed to show him greatly in advance of Vice-President Humphrey, the administration's candidate, McCarthy seemed to lose interest in the antiwar movement to which he had given such impetus. The casual way in which he commented on the Soviet invasion of Czechoslovakia called his judgment into question. The McCarthy movement—indeed, the whole movement known as the "New Politics"—became a vehicle for reform of the Democratic party. In Chicago the unit rule of voting was abolished and a sweeping democratization of delegate selection was instituted for the future. Such reform was much needed: in Pennsylvania, for instance, McCarthy won 75 percent of the primary vote but received only 25 percent of the delegates. In sum, McCarthy's was a protest movement as much as a serious try for the presidency. Even in its own terms it was an aberration; while McCarthy's air of intellect and cold virtue had its attractions for the educated young, it neither bespoke nor called upon the passions needed for a sustained political uprising.

But McCarthy was not oblivious to political necessity. Mayor Daley of Chicago encouraged a last-minute effort to seize the nomination from Humphrey and give it to the first family's surviving brother, Senator Edward Kennedy of Massachusetts, who had the support of California, New York, Massachusetts, and perhaps Illinois, Michigan, and many other large states. McCarthy offered to withdraw in Kennedy's favor. The attempt depended on the psychology of the national political convention, where an image of losing projected upon Humphrey and one of strength fastened to Kennedy could change the thinking of many delegates overnight. Thousands of young people demonstrating outside in the streets against Johnson and Vietnam were a powerful reminder that perhaps, after all, Humphrey would not do. But Edward Kennedy, implored to run, finally took himself out of consideration. He apparently believed that he was not sufficiently seasoned, at thirty-six, to be President, and no doubt the assassination of his brother Robert had shocked him.

Without leadership, the peace contingent dissolved. It had lost by a decisive 3-to-2 vote an attempt to insert a platform provision calling for a halt to all bombing in Vietnam. The mood of despair communicated itself to the thousands of young people gathered outside in Grant Park when the nominating speeches were made. Repelled by the protesters' styles, the Chicago police, in what a government report later termed a "police riot," turned violently against the young. Inside the hall, Senator Abraham Ribicoff of Connecticut, hearing of the violence, struck out at the "Gestapo tactics" on the streets of Chicago. Daley leapt to his feet and barked unequivocal language at Ribicoff. After the riot Hubert Humphrey's nomination, by a margin of 2-to-1 over McCarthy and Senator George McGovern, the other peace candidate, was anticlimactic. That night the police invaded some McCarthy student suites in the convention hotel. Chicago, which Martin Luther King, Jr., had called the "most segregated city of the North," now stood for violence as it had in the 1920s. The Mayor himself, during the riots after the King assassination, had set the tone by his widely reported order: "Shoot to kill arsonists and shoot to maim looters." Americans who watched the convention on television were left with an impression of violence and turmoil, which also pursued Humphrey on his early campaign trips.

It is hard to fathom the Hubert Humphrey of 1968, proclaiming the "politics of joy" at a time when the social fabric was almost torn apart. Yet he was a man with a good past. The Peace Corps and Medicare were mainly his ideas. He had worked for federal aid to education as early as the 1940s, and at the Democratic Convention of 1948 he had been willing to split the party over civil rights, which earlier he had worked for as mayor of Minneapolis. But when he was asked as Vice-President what had happened to the liberal program he had once stood for, he answered: "We passed it." He criticized blacks for not making the economic advances the Irish and Italians had; and he ridiculed Mayor John Lindsay's police review board. If issues were that simple to him, his career showed indeed the exhaustion of a liberalism that might otherwise have moved to a genuine left-of-center politics.

While Vice-President, Humphrey maintained an unrelenting, rigid anticommunism. In a mystical flight of rhetoric during 1967 he called the threat to peace in Vietnam "a militant, aggressive Asian communism with headquarters in Peking." Years before he had sponsored the Communist Control Act of 1954, outlawing the Communist party in America, and offered an amendment to allow setting up concentration camps for Communists during times of national emergency. In opposition to President Eisenhower's requests, he had consistently supported huge military budgets, and he had suggested giving the CIA a billion dollars to carry on its varied activities. Until business interests persuaded him otherwise, he had opposed trading surplus farm products with Iron Curtain countries.

As one of the few Johnson administration spokesmen who sought to articulate a justification for the Vietnam war, Humphrey sometimes lapsed into absurdity. He told University of Pittsburgh students that only the Vietcong had committed atrocities. He announced to the AFL-CIO that those who called for peace in Vietnam were kin to those who said we should make peace with Hitler after his forces had rolled across the lowlands. If South Vietnam was corrupt, he observed, so were some American cities. Above all, he repeatedly charged that the Chinese Communists were directing the war. The very act of support for his President in Vietnam drew Humphrey's energies away from domestic reform.

The prospect of Humphrey as nominee dismayed antiwar Democrats. The Republicans, of course, did not have the hard job of explaining the Vietnam war, and it was clear that they held a strong political position. At first liberal Republicans looked to Governor George Romney of Michigan, a strong proponent of civil rights. But Romney tended to be a bit too open for the political life: in September 1967 he casually remarked that on an early visit to Vietnam he had succumbed to a "brainwashing" given him by briefing officers. After poor showings in early polls, Romney decided to withdraw from the race.

Another liberal, Governor Nelson Rockefeller of New York, belatedly declared his candidacy on April 30, 1968, and proceeded to spend almost five million dollars on a media campaign to get himself nominated. The only specifically right-wing candidate, Governor Ronald Reagan of California, played a cautious hand, privately available and promoted by a low-pressure television campaign, but publicly out of

the race. Both governors knew that the only way to keep the nomination away from former Vice-President Richard Nixon, the sole
candidate in the political center and the strongest contestant—his
victories in the spring contests had freed him from his reputation
for being a loser—was to encourage favorite son candidacies and
collect as many votes as possible to prevent him from winning on the
first ballot. They nearly succeeded in causing an upset at Miami.
Reagan was extremely popular in the South and would have made
serious incursions there but for the powerful influence of Senator
Strom Thurmond, who supported Nixon after assurance from the
candidate that he would heed the South. Rockefeller put his hopes
in the preconvention polls, but they did not give him what he needed,
some clear statement that he would be the most effective nominee.
Nixon needed only 667 votes to win, and he received 691.

Richard Nixon was real Americana. He had grown up playing the
piano at church, cranking home-made ice cream at parties, and excel-
ling on the high school debating team, and during his navy years he
set up a hamburger stand in the South Pacific, and saved a considerable sum won in poker. He earned his way through Whittier College
and Duke University Law School. Skills in debating and poker, as
well as legal training, were good preparation for a political career.

Much has been made of Nixon's red-baiting when he won
a House seat in 1946 and advanced to the Senate in 1950. Even as late
as 1954, after he had campaigned hard for Republican congressmen,
Adlai Stevenson labeled him a "white-collar McCarthy." Nixon certainly won votes by portraying his opponents as indifferent to communism; he had, after all, conducted the public investigation of Alger
Hiss, accused of having been a Communist agent in the 1930s. And
Murray Chotiner, as campaign director in 1946, employed the crassest
materialism, giving "BIG PRIZES" to win support for Nixon. But
the 1950 campaign was crude on both sides, and Nixon himself was
charged with anti-Semitism and fascism.

During his career in the national legislature Nixon accumulated
a mixed voting record, conservative and liberal by fits, often solici-
tous of civil liberties and sometimes not. He was an early supporter
of Dwight Eisenhower for President, preferring him to the more conservative Senator Robert Taft, whom he thought the weaker candidate. Nixon's fame in the Hiss investigation, his strength in California
and his influence with its convention delegates, his nondescript voting record and service in both House and Senate—all cast him as a
strong vice-presidential candidate in 1952, and Governor Tom Dewey
of New York, who had the ear of Eisenhower, put him across.

Weathering an unfair charge of corruption made during the 1952
campaign, Nixon went on to become an effective Vice-President,

although Eisenhower never appreciated his political talent. In the 1950s Nixon promoted civil rights as vigorously as any politician was doing. His own Quaker ancestors had been active in nineteenth-century antislavery agitation. Nixon had been a member of the NAACP since 1950, and as late as August 1960 Eleanor Roosevelt praised Nixon's Committee on Government Contracts for doing a good job in promoting nondiscriminatory hiring. After losing to Kennedy in 1960 Nixon returned to his legal residence in California, where in 1962 he lost another close election, for the governorship of that state. He survived the Goldwater debacle very well, while moderate Republicans who had not given full support to the candidate were losing favor with party leaders. After California he moved to New York City, distinguishing himself in law practice by appearing on two occasions before the Supreme Court in an argument for the right to privacy (*Time, Inc.* v. *Hill* [1966]): But this case was taken on in part to show that he believed in such procedural rights, for in 1965 Nixon had denounced a Rutgers University professor, Eugene Genovese, who had said he would welcome a Vietcong victory; such a statement, Nixon declared in supporting an attempt to dismiss Genovese, was not admissible in wartime. Nixon later took more care, avoiding hard statements on Vietnam. In 1968 he seemed more relaxed and at ease with himself than ever before. After the Miami Convention his presidential campaign proceeded cautiously, intent on keeping the large Nixon lead over Humphrey in the polls.

By contrast the Humphrey campaign, inaugurated so dismally in Chicago, continued a disaster all through September. The administration was a terrible burden on Humphrey. His promise of an early end to the war was contradicted by a statement from Dean Rusk, not long after, that no one could predict when the war's pace might slacken. Antiwar hecklers pursued Humphrey everywhere, and perhaps had some role in forcing him to reconsider his position on Vietnam. In a nationwide television speech on September 30, he dissociated himself from the administration by calling for an immediate halt to all bombing of North Vietnam. From that point on the polls showed the gap between Humphrey and Nixon steadily narrowing.

Meanwhile, Governor George Wallace of Alabama and his American Independent party had launched the most ambitious third-party campaign since Robert La Follette's forty-four years before. Wallace's initial popularity in the South was built upon a simple campaign slogan: "Segregation now—Segregation tomorrow—Segregation forever." But the governor's following expanded in the course of the decade. Chief Justice Earl Warren of the Supreme Court was to be impeached not only for *Brown* v. *Board of Education*, but also for decisions outlawing school prayers, protecting the rights of accused criminals, dictating a "one man, one vote" representative system, and strengthening further the civil rights of black citizens. The Wallace campaign was primarily about the racial issue, but the candidate also inveighed against "bearded bureaucrats," "pointy-headed professors," "sissy-britches," and "poor-folks haters"; for his campaign was something like a class movement, called forth by the divisions in education and style and values that have replaced wealth as the social differentia. All of the rancor that burned in the Wallace supporters was caught in the menacing slogan of "law and order." Wallace's presence in the campaign meant that Nixon too could preach law and order and yet maintain himself as a centrist candidate. Wallace, who had found a place on the ballot in every state, was running a good race in late September when the Gallup Poll credited him with as much as 20 percent of the vote. But his share of the electorate declined all through October, with Humphrey the beneficiary. Labor unions, hoping to aid their traditional allies in the Democratic party, spent record amounts to portray Wallace as unfriendly to labor. And the labor campaign hit home; Alabama was indeed a low-wage, open-shop state. What irritated Wallace most of all were groups of long-haired boys and girls who pretended to be on his side, sometimes shouting "Sieg heil, y'all." Wallace's vice-presidential candidate, General Curtis LeMay, had his own special outlook. "We seem to have a phobia about nuclear weapons," LeMay said in language reminiscent of Barry Goldwater's. "I don't believe the world would end if we exploded a nuclear weapon."

Nixon's vice-presidential running mate, Governor Spiro Agnew of Maryland, was inept in national politics. Agnew, who had campaigned for the governorship on an open-housing platform, and at a time when the issue was a dangerous one in Maryland politics, had nonetheless found himself as governor in a series of confrontations with black leaders and demands, and he had behaved with a closed-minded assurance that southern politicians found to their taste. Though he was in fact more a frustrated liberal on the racial question than a conservative, he was selected for the national ticket as an inducement to the South. He proceeded awkwardly. Vernacular jokes about "polacks" and "that fat Jap," which he had not meant to be insulting, helped not at all. And after he told reporters that Humphrey had been "soft on communism," he said he would not have used the phrase had he known its "political history." Democrats ran a television ad mentioning Agnew, followed by uproarious laughter; another one showed his face and played the sound of a beating heart, raising the specter of President Agnew. Humphrey's running mate, Senator Edmund Muskie of Maine, conducted a quietly effective campaign calculated to reassure traditional Democratic voters among labor and foreign-born groups.

Humphrey came very close to winning the election. In late October, Hanoi and the Allies agreed to peace talks in Paris, and the bombing of North Vietnam ceased; had these things come a bit sooner, Humphrey would have become President. But Nixon was lucky in 1968 as he had been unlucky in 1960. Nothing like the television debates of 1960 happened to him; and at one point at least he profited from an act of reticence on the part of his foe. Humphrey would have won if he had not decided to refrain from publicizing the efforts of Mrs. Anna Chennault, a co-chairwoman of the Republican campaign, to hold up South Vietnamese acceptance of peace talks. As it was, Nixon won by almost as close a margin as Kennedy had possessed over him at the beginning of the decade. Humphrey won some 88 percent of the Negro vote and even more of the Mexican-American. None of the largest cities went to the Republican party, and it did not gain Congress: it advanced its strength by only four seats in the House and five in the Senate. There was no clearly discernible trend away from the Democratic majorities that had generally prevailed since the New Deal.

But the margin of votes does not measure the meaning of the election for the liberal forces. The real prize had slipped from them months and years before: an articulate conception of what liberalism was now to be, armed with a language to give that conception passionate force. And it was not the fault of the liberals. Vice-President Humphrey's generation could not easily have thought its way outside the older terms of the welfare state, the trust in centralized programs heavily administered from Washington and received with cooperation by the people they served; New Dealers had fought for this kind of reform, seen it triumph, and built upon it to the impressive though incomplete structures of the Great Society. For Humphrey to have attempted a vocabulary fitted to an era of black power, the universities of the street, and all the peculiar compounds we have seen of hard reformism with communalist or existential imagination would have required some violence to his own past—and lost him many votes. Perhaps his failure to speak to 1968 reflected a certain integrity. But it must have been a lonely failure; for it also denied him the satisfaction of other things his liberalism was founded in—an identity with the major currents of militant enthusiasm, and an empathy with the dispossessed.

Nixon as President was at first slow to acquire a political coloration. Abortive attempts to raise the conservative southern Judges Carswell and Haynsworth to the Supreme Court suggest simple reaction as much as a cynical appeal to the white South. The caustic rhetoric of Vice-President Agnew gives the administration distinctive tone. The "incursion" into Cambodia was justified by Nixon for the worst of all reasons: he said he did not want to be the first American President to preside over a military defeat. On the other hand, this has not been a hard-rightist administration. It has proceeded with the policy Johnson had begun of a slow disengagement from Vietnam. William Rogers has been a temperate Secretary of State; Melvin Laird has supervised sharp curtailments of military expenditures in the Department of Defense; former Secretary Walter Hickel of the Interior Department, who had once been thought a conservative, drew attention when he called for openness toward the disaffected young. It can even be argued that the South is improving its record of school desegregation more willingly for Attorney General John Mitchell than it might have under a Robert Kennedy. Former Secretary of Health, Education, and Welfare Robert Finch, now an adviser to the President, has kept liberal welfare legislation alive, although such a strong liberal as Commissioner of Education James Allen was fired. Richard Nixon is a very political man, hoping to build up his support in the conservative South and the small states of the West but always aware that, while he can lose the East and still win reelection, he must capture a majority in several large industrial states.

Within these states Richard Nixon has known well which voters are most receptive to him. Nixon's "Middle America" includes not only traditional Republicans but also the beleaguered lower-middle-income voters especially of the denser suburbs. These hard-working Americans, many of them registered Democrats and still possessed of a distinct ethnic identity, have worried much about their future— the prospect of competing with black men in the labor market and watching their neighborhoods go to another race they have feared, of being nibbled down by inflation, of having their children learn values alien to theirs. It seems appropriate that Nixon was occupying the White House when three young Americans landed on the moon in the summer of 1969, and that he should greet the clean-cut astronauts after they splashed home in the Pacific; here were heroes, and genuine ones, for the country that middle America wants to believe in. Other Americans regarded the moon landing with indifference or skepticism: blacks saw no brothers among the astronauts and they noted the priority that the moon was getting over the ghettos; middle-class urban and suburban liberals questioned why the moon venture should be more important than the poverty measures its funds might have supplied; and the coldly mechanical triumph held no grip on the disaffected young.

In an earlier period of history the administration might possibly have been classed as mildly liberal. Its foreign policy looks to detente, it makes at least public efforts toward integration and probably means them, and it has proposed the most advanced welfare system Washington has ever lengthily considered. Yet it gets its tenor from other facts, some of them having to do not with specific programs but with subtler matters of gesture and identity; they signify the extent to which style and language, and beneath them deeper shapes of culture, are controlling political questions of the present. The administration, which is very happy to find that it is conservative and has done much to confirm the fact, is nevertheless conservative in part through new definitions and circumstances. If the Nixon government represents the defeat of liberalism, one reason is that it embodies much of a liberalism pushed to contrariness.

Spiro Agnew is a good example. He is not a red-baiter or a segregationist, and he should be remembered for his advocacy of open housing for Maryland. The enemy he has now defined for himself is Permissiveness, and while for several decades liberalism has looked more favorably on philosophies of child freedom, tolerance for deviant behavior, and free expression even of distasteful material than conservatism has, the issue had never translated itself into national political terms. It now has, with the help of the Vice-President, who is quite honest in his indignations—some of the acts he dislikes are obnoxious to any civilized taste—and who is quite possibly angry that so many efforts and institutions of liberal reform have met only assault from the militants and the student left. His campaign is part of a larger battle that pits Woodstock against the older decorous assemblages of the middle class, that makes the academic argument for and against grades and established curricula practically a test of political ideologies, and that has given us the metaphysical debate over hair. And all this is a real issue, for important points about the uses of forms and the qualities of experience are involved, but it is terribly inarticulate and distorted.

Actually, the nation by the end of the decade had broken into many subcultures. That fact of itself does not set the period off from earlier times. But the subcultures are remarkably self-aware and belligerent, and at the same time the distinctions among them are often in details and nuances. Liberals generally belong to a university culture rather than to a broad middle class. Old people are less and less old businessmen or old workers or old Democrats or old Catholics; they have become oldsters, living in their own communities and concerned about their particular collective interests. Students are not simply apprentices to a variety of roles but a consciously distinct force. Hippies practice one kind of cultural separatism, and some black militants another. Conservatives have ceased being a wing of a party and have turned into a separate pressure group, and almost a culture to themselves. Even the "silent majority" looks less like a majority, inclusive of differences, than like another subculture.

The subcultures can be confusingly overlapped among themselves or divided within. The colleges and universities are the enclave of a special culture in which students, faculty, and administration participate in different ways. Yet the students are distinct from the rest. On the other hand, they share traits with some young people outside the campuses. The new workers pouring into the giant Ford plant at River Rouge, for example, wear love beads and beards, turn down requests to work overtime, and lack the acquisitive instinct of the older workers on the line. Management frankly confesses that it has not yet found out how to motivate them—and the deans of many colleges can sympathize. Union leaders are likely to have at least as bad a time.

Some of the churches, traditional bulwarks of the "American way" that Will Herberg in the 1950s found to be our official religion, have also spun away. The bureaucratic elaboration of the churches (following the course of other American institutions) has aided in creating a new breed of church liberals. Clergymen free of congregational control over their salaries and their conduct—denomination and interdenominational staff people, college chaplains, and ministers of urban mission churches—have been heavily represented in the civil rights movement and in efforts to aid and organize the urban poor. Many churches serve as sponsors for the schemes of community organization connected with the poverty program; but after 1965 the major denominations suffered a decline in membership gain and a loss in revenue.

One of the more recent fragmentings has been the sudden assertive self-awareness among a number of American women. By the end of the decade women's rights groups were springing up, the media were filled with discussions, a women's rights amendment to the Constitution was passed by the House of Representatives after years of fruitless submission, and books on the plight of women were making the best seller lists. This revival of an old dormant cause was sparked by Betty Friedan's *The Feminine Mystique*, published in 1963, an attack on the cult of home, children, and sex. Soon afterward she organized NOW, the National Organization of Women, which lobbied for reform of abortion laws, for child-care facilities, and most of all for equal employment opportunities. Then in about 1967 women's rights assumed fresh belligerency. Much of it came from women radicals who had discovered that they were being exploited by radicalism exactly as bourgeois women were used—as cooks, secretaries, and bed partners. The new activists look to issues beyond the social and economic ones of the early days; waging war against what Kate

Millett called "sexual politics," they seek to transform the place and image of women within the culture. They have been especially perceptive about the "sexual revolution," which they claim has not freed woman but simply made her more available. They resent advertisements presenting women as "sexual objects"; they especially denounce advertising that sets women into sexual competition with one another; the new explicitness in pictures and movies, they protest, reduces women to subjects of display.

Women's liberation is related to a failure that has extended to American radicalism. In radical politics, the women found, they were still making the coffee and taking the notes while the men strutted and posed, planned and directed. Among the hippies, the rejection of work carried with it hidden cultural assumptions taken from American society: the rejection was of what America defines as work, jobs that men hold and are paid for. All the other kinds of work that women daily perform without any status or claim to vocation went on, and in many hippie communes women did all the chores and remained caught in the feminine mystique. The image of men and women in the rock world has been shocking by enlightened standards. The groupie culture is a study in female degradation, and the new sexual freedom has spawned a cult of male sexuality that both the lives and the lyrics of the leading singers profusely illustrate. Rock music has been overwhelmingly a male domain in which women performers have no more of a place than women did in middle-class culture. One of the great female rock stars, the late Janis Joplin, worked for a group called "Big Brother and the Holding Company," and women have been heavily represented only in the fields of folk music (Joan Baez and Judy Collins) and specifically black or "Soul" music (Dionne Warwicke and Aretha Franklin). In the film *Alice's Restaurant*, an honest and thoughtful evocation of the youth culture, women are either cooks or rejected sexual objects.

The radical women's liberation movement is to a considerable extent a recoil from a situation within radical culture. But it is better described as one of the angers awakened from radicalism, which is among other things a progression into anger. Radicalism of all kinds has had much to do with the fragmenting of American civilization, and is itself of fragments.

Landscape by Tom McCarthy.

"Once upon a time there lived a little green elf in an old oak tree which had been condemned to make way for Interstate 95. The old oak tree stood by contaminated waters that ran along the edge of the strip mine just twenty-five miles from the heavily polluted air of the city. In spite of his emphysema he was a fairly happy elf ..."

Cartoon by Henry Martin.

Congestion, U.S.A., 1960s. (Arthur Tress)

Mangrove forests in Vietnam before and after defoliation. (UPI)

Record cover by MC Productions and The Apple. (Courtesy Capitol Records)

Scenes at Woodstock Festival, White Lake, N.Y., 1969. (Ken Heyman)

Jimi Hendrix. (UPI)   Janis Joplin. (College Newsphoto Alliance)

George Wallace. (Richard Howard, Bethel)

Easy Rider. (UPI)

Timothy Leary, "The Illumination of the Buddha." (Fred McDarrah)

Police march off Harvard campus after dispersing students. (Editorial Photocolor Archives)

Student and police conflict at San Francisco State College. Students tried to stop military recruiters from operating at school. (Wide World)

Marchers in conservative rally led by Rev. Carl McIntyre in support of U.S. involvement in the Vietnam war. (College Newsphoto Alliance)

A member of the Third World. (Editorial Photocolor Archives)

Cesar Chavez voices protest over Defense Department's purchase of nonunion lettuce outside Fort Hamilton Army Base, New York. (Hap Stewart)

Leslie Fiedler, author of *Being Busted*. (Diana Davies, Bethel)

Ohio National Guard members ascend hill at Kent State University shortly before they fired upon students. (UPI)

Construction workers protest, New York City. (Charles Gatewood)

Joan Baez talks about income taxes and the Vietnam war. (Mark Chester, ASCAP)

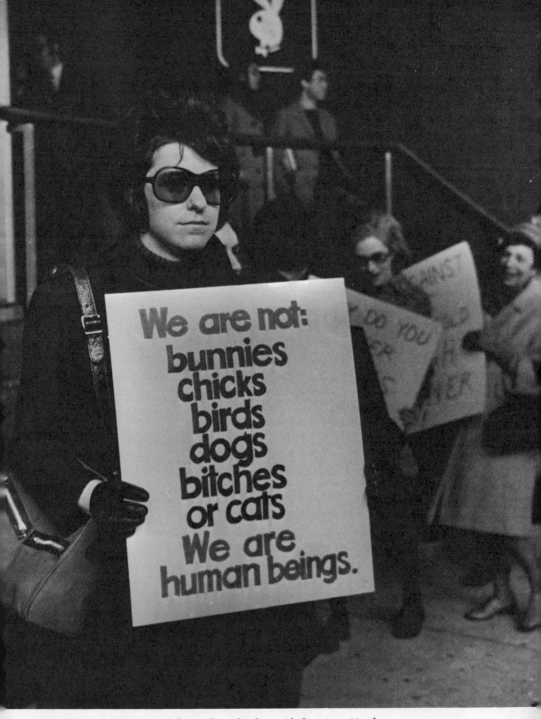

Women's Liberation pickets the Playboy Club, New York. (Diana Davies, Bethel)

Earth Day participant, New York. (John C. Goodwin)

Twiggy. (Bert Stern photograph from VOGUE; Copyright © 1967 by The Conde Nast Publications, Inc.)

Cartoon by Herblock.

'What ! Add a $10 gadget like that ?'

Landscape by Tom McCarthy.

a radical intuition

The later 1960s have been prolific of radical strains and movements, each with its distinctive character. Some of the cultural radicals are antipolitical, keeping aloof from the programs on the Left that they think would intrude, as much as conventional culture does, upon the free pursuit of intuition or of community. A number of political militants, especially in the mid-sixties, explicitly shunned the ways of the new culture for being self-indulgent and corrosive of the discipline and persistence that activism must possess. The artistic ventures that appear so much akin to the rest of radicalism in their revolutionary energies, the hard rock, the experimental films, and the participatory theater, must be critically appreciated on artistic grounds, each of them by reference to the distinctive techniques in which it works.

Nevertheless, observers have found in much of

the new radicalism an element of consistency. Speaking especially of the cultural as opposed to the more narrowly political phenomena of dissent, Theodore Roszak has given a broad description in his sympathetic and perceptive *The Making of a Counter Culture*. He defines the new culture as a revolt against the "objective consciousness," the mind of the technocracy, of the rational scientists, engineers, and statesmen who manage our lives, coldly examining and arranging the objects of the world rather than feeling for them as having independence and mystery. The quest for a new culture now has another forceful definition, given in Charles Reich's *The Greening of America*. It is a naive book, deliberately so, but its freshness and detail make their own argument. The title elegantly catches the quality that Reich finds in what he calls "Consciousness III," green and living with sensibility, sprouting in a land that had been the sterile domain of the technocratic consciousness.

The "consciousness" that both authors set out to describe can best be understood not so much as a single state of mind as a composite of experience that has been sought for the integrity, the brilliance, or the enlightenment they may hold. These experiences are of no single kind. Some of the cultural radicals have explored mysticism and the reaches of the imagination; some have desired experience that is clear, plain, and tactile, gotten with simple living and manual work; some pursue community and the perfecting of love. The means can be as diverse as the objectives, and they may be drawn from the present environment: its politics, purged and reshaped; several of its occupations; its universities; even its rationalism. And there need be no one dominant attitude toward modern technology, which on the one hand threatens experience and on the other provides instruments for vivid achievements and reconstructions of it. The counterculture does not really center in the dramatic events and movements that the media have fastened upon; it is carried out in a number of small personal choices. Any analysis of it will be abstract and incomplete: its essence escapes through the pores of language.

The new culture has ancient antecedents. The command to put off the old self and receive a regenerate one is at the core of Western culture, as deep as the rationalist tradition of the West. Christianity has carried a new consciousness that has periodically broken through the cold shell of the commonsensical world and realized itself in mysticism, in monastic communities and pietistic sects, in art and liturgy; and that new consciousness sits in perpetual judgment upon the Christian. The social vision of the cultural Left has at least one fairly close predecessor in the special strain of radicalism, appearing in later nineteenth-century Britain through the work of John Ruskin, William Morris, and others, that would combine socialism with the feeling, the community, and the free craftsmanship its spokesmen associated with medieval times. More immediately, the counterculture is an unfolding out of some things it opposes. When liberalism came fully to the issue of civil rights, it released in itself a moral passion and a vision of community that could not rest within the conventional temper and solutions of liberalism. The revolution in the universities has been a natural development from the virtues they have taught—relentless inquiry and the breaking of established intellectual forms. At the instant when the new culture appeared ready for a full expression of itself, the ground for it having been prepared by the beats and by the civil rights movement, the environment seemed to stiffen. At a time when a certain kind of student was looking for a sensitive and informal community of learning, the university was visibly accelerating its expansion into the impersonal multiversity. Civil rights, after initial triumphs over particularly vicious and explicit—but for that reason particularly vulnerable— racist institutions, came up against less identifiable and more frustrating problems of economics and hidden racism. And then, of course, there was Vietnam. Without the particular tempos of social advances and social failures during the early and middle sixties radical culture would perhaps not have come into being, or would have remained at a private fringe of American society. It would be a mistake, though, to search too closely for specific facts of American life that have driven the cultural insurrectionists into "alienation." They are perfectionist and angry; in the face of their absolute and often their arrogant demands, any society will seem to be a pitiable affair of dishonesties, mediocre labor, and muddy compromises. To this extent the new culture is an event in the continuing conscience that civilization bears against its own imperfection.

The new radicalism is, however, in another sense very much of our own time. While it may be definable as a rebellion against the cold logic of machine civilization, it is also definable as a product of that civilization, as having in its being a knowledge of form and logic that makes possible by dialectical opposition the experience of release from logic. Modern technology, in fact, lends something more direct of itself to that liberation from the bounds of logic. For while in one of its modes it is rationalist, in another it has achieved extreme rearrangements of the rationalist universe: in the modern media it has made space vanish, and in the technology of the film it has thrown together clashing images, broken and reformed the sequences; and the imagination of the counterculture can draw upon these things. Progressive rock has made use of electricity. And this music has a deeper resonance with technology: it has sounds as hard as metal, fragments like well-shaped pieces of steel, and when they are put together into driven patterns they suggest the fragmentation and tempo of some industrial landscape, even as the music dissolves the fragments into a vital and electrical fluency. Rock may in truth owe little to the machine directly besides electric sound and amplification; but many of its tones, which go quite compatibly with the folkish notes that echo in it, make it an appropriate music for its age. In all the connections the radical culture has with technology—its dialectical recoil from technical logic into free experience, and its more cooperative relations—it gains a sophistication it might not recognize or acknowledge in itself.

Seeking purification and wholeness of experience, the new culture exists between opposite possibilities. Some of its members want experience in a primal state, and make the implicit claim that the true consciousness will come not through controlled awareness but through the rejection of form, and by a sheer opening to consciousness. At times its political morality subsists on a boundless and undiscriminating anger, as though the making of distinctions would destroy the purity of the moral emotions. But the radical culture also has a bent for disciplined experience. Much taste and craftsmanship exist, and especially a sensitivity to shapes and colors even in such details as mural and poster decoration. In music and some other arts the new culture has made distinctive technical accomplishments. While it has a strong streak of anti-intellectualism, it has an interest in mental pursuit of an esoteric and often a complicated kind, in which the intellect bends materials out of their old formal contours into some abrupt new configuration. This double tendency, on the one hand toward spontaneity and on the other toward precision of experience, should provide a good base for an examination of the new culture in a few of its expressions.

In the sixties, the older collegiate society of fraternities and intercollegiate athletics was being undermined by a new emphasis on merit and intellectuality on the one hand, and on the university's functioning in the larger world on the other. College as pastoral interlude was apparently dying.

Stephen Spender, observing the young rebels at the 1968 Democratic Convention in Chicago, was struck by their advance of two or three years in maturity over that possessed by his college generation of the thirties. Psychological tests taken over a period of years indicate that almost every class of freshmen from the early fifties to the late sixties has been at a higher level of sophistication. Politically or culturally creative students are a tiny fraction of the student population; but they are drawn together by their inclination toward the social sciences and humanities. During the fifties, to the contrary, it had been the scientists, affected by the politics of nuclear weapons, who were the vanguard of whatever campus radicalism there was. And the potential activists are further concentrated by their presence in honors classes, seminars, or the more intellectual extracurricular activities, for before the movement gained a penumbra of faddists, it was determinably the domain of the best students.

The student movement of the early sixties was grounded partly in American liberalism and partly in the old Left. The brief student participation in the peace movement between 1961 and 1963, its origins in the Berlin crisis and its demise in the signing of the nuclear Test Ban Treaty, was through organs of the old radicalism, the student auxiliary of SANE and an offshoot of the Socialist party. In civil rights the students worked partly within a strategy of law and jurisprudence that came from the previous decade and earlier. Even the Student Nonviolent Coordinating Committee, which drew a good portion of the radicals among the activists, originated in the liberal civil rights movement and maintained some relations with it through the early part of the decade. The style of the students—blue jeans, jeans jacket, and sunglasses—was distinctive, and their hope for a regenerate community bespoke the advent of a very special sensibility. But the students abided by the old liberal canons, and something of the respect for institutional forms.

The first group to advance with any success beyond a single issue such as peace or civil rights was the Students for a Democratic Society (SDS), which in the course of the decade came closer than any other organization to being at the center of the amorphous and leaderless student Left. SDS was a continuation of an old socialist youth group, the Student League for Industrial Democracy. Although close to moribund in the forties and fifties, SLID had maintained some radical éclat by virtue of distinguished and able leaders in the fifties, such as James Farmer, who later led and radicalized CORE, and Gabriel Kolko, a prolific and talented young historian. In 1960, with the rebirth of student activism, SLID acquired a new name and soon a new character. Two activists at the University of Michigan, Al Haber and Tom Hayden, pressed to render SDS a genuinely nationwide organization devoted to a general radical program rather than to specific objectives defined by events and the national administration.Their effort stirred enough interest on other campuses to make a national convention feasible. This convention, held at a United Auto Workers center in Port Huron, Michigan, approved a manifesto drafted by Hayden, "The Port Huron Statement," which became the first intellectual landmark of the student Left—an "agenda for a generation," its opening claimed.

The wide success of the document among students—it launched SDS—can be attributed to its mixture of generality and honesty. "We are the people of this generation," it began, "bred in at least modest comfort, housed now in universities, looking uncomfortably to the world we inherit." This is strange language for a revolutionary manifesto. The call is to renovate existing institutions. The plight of the Negro is examined in carefully ordered statistics and shrewd analysis of political strategies. The document describes the condition of the students in modest terms, and the possibilities of the university as a base for radicalism is broached as a new idea needing prudent development. The rhetoric is the language of social science. Yet the main notes are there: the insistence on an end to international tension, the rejection of anticommunism as an ideology, the antagonism to bureaucracy, the desire to overcome alienation and helplessness, to achieve community and a true politics, the search for a student identity and a place of power in modern life.

For the next two years, SDS and the student movement remained an appendage of the civil rights movement. Many white youths experienced the dangers of rights work in the South, and frustration at the insufficiency of their peaceful tactics. They also learned to distrust the national administration for its failure to protect them. The students' model, SNCC, was going through important changes as it gradually ceased cooperating with the liberal coalition—especially after the final rejection of the Mississippi Freedom contingent by the Democratic party nationally—and turned to "participatory democracy" for the poor as its alternative to liberal compromise. SDS tried to imitate the efforts of SNCC with community organization in the North, only to discover—as the Johnson administration would later—the difficulty of community organization in areas where there was in fact no community. And the young radicals were learning how antithetical was "participatory democracy" to liberalism, which emphasizes expertise, bureaucracy, and general nationwide regulation.

The most graphic lessons in participatory democracy and its relationship to liberalism were available at the students' home base in the university. The universities, in their management, ideology, and personnel, were by far the most liberal institutions in the country. Even before the student revolts of the decade, they were among the only places radical speakers could get a hall and a hearing, and they were the leading patrons of avant-garde art. The more prestigious institutions such as Berkeley and the University of Wisconsin had spawned a bohemian or nonstudent fringe.

At Berkeley a restriction on campus recruiting for off-campus political activity, mostly in civil rights, set off a student movement that paralyzed the campus for months and sent tremors through academia that have yet to be stilled. The administration had wanted to do this without unnecessarily provoking students, and it offered compromise after compromise on the issue in order to demonstrate that it was engaged in no plot against the students' rights of free speech or political association. It had no reason to doubt the validity, legal and moral, of its position. What it found, however, was that negotiating with students was a dangerous business, damaging to some unstated assumptions upon which the university operated. The established academic community did not think that the university should play a political role; the students thought that it implicitly did. The administrators and faculty reasoned that the university was a place not for activism but for learning: "I don't think you have to have action to have intellectual opportunity," said the President, Clark Kerr; and the students argued that their activities for civil rights were the principal element of their education. The university believed in regulations, the radical students in participatory democracy. The university worked with established bureaucratic procedures; the students had already been trained to demonstrations.

Yet for all this, the students at Berkeley and elsewhere had touched the academic conscience. The cry for student power brought up questions of how much power the faculty exercised in a giant institution like the University of California system; in attacking the impersonality and computerization of the campus, the rebels were attacking a vice that stubborn academic conservatism and elegant traditionalism cannot abide either; the demand for a more open curriculum could rest on the old commitment to imaginative inquiry; the moral call to address the problems of the society beyond the campus was an embarrassment to professors who were liberal but hesitant to burden the university with outside involvement.

The assault on the moral authority of the universities was logical, for they had become powers in the land. Even the leadership of faculties in opposing the Vietnam war did not prevent the student movements from fastening some complicity for it on the universities. Research sponsored by the Department of Defense, recruiting on campus by the military and by corporations like Dow Chemical that made napalm, and the presence of ex-academics in major government roles, all gave support to the argument of the radicals that the universities were parts of the power structure leading America on adventures in Asia and elsewhere. Universities had cooperated, usually with some caution, on intelligence and military projects sometimes of dubious intellectual value and had even tolerated classified research—which goes against the academic value of free inquiry. Many of the most sophisticated apologists for American foreign policy were in the universities, and the campuses directly trained those who staffed every branch of the "establishment."

In a very special way the university was vulnerable. Two administrators will serve as illustration. The crucially important relationship of the university to the larger world has been starkly delineated by the University of California's Clark Kerr, first casualty of the student wars; the acknowledgment that universities were not democratic institutions was bluntly made by Herbert Deane, Dean of Faculties, during the critical times in 1968 at Columbia. The noticeable thing here is the candor. In no other institution would administrators have provided the weapons for their opponents. By the time a serious scholar becomes an administrator, however, he will have developed, as these men had, a habit of trying to tell the truth. Indeed, if he does not, his evasions are somehow far less forgivable than the ones routinely expected from other men stalking the corridors of power; and this suggests another element in the peculiar vulnerability of the schools. American society has throughout the twentieth century applied standards far more perfectionist to its educational systems than to any other; it would not tolerate in any other major institutions the endless reorganizings and experimentings that education has gone through, nor would it be so angered at evidence that the personnel are, after all, human and faltering. The rigid integrity that the students demand of their universities is deeply within the American credo. Disillusionment with higher education had particularly important consequences, for the universities were the last institutional link binding the affluent but disaffected young to their society.

Many faculty members joined with the students, while others condemned the student demands for threatening the liberal function of the university, study and discourse. Perhaps the most positive response at the large universities was to ride the student movements in hopes of leading them toward desirable university reforms. For a few years, coalitions of liberal faculty and radical students had great effect in reforming the universities to more innovative teaching and curricula and to some freedom from their expanded bureaucracies. "Don't trust anyone over 30," Mario Savio advised in 1964. Now he and many other student radicals are past the formidable birthday. Some Americans may find it comforting to suppose that young radicals grow into "mature" liberals or conservatives. But by the end of the decade, ex-students were busy trying to radicalize the professions and scholarly disciplines they had entered. Professional meetings—from those of the bar associations and the AMA to historical, sociological, and scientific congregations—had their radical caucuses pressing the student message that even the activity most apparently neutral has political content, that inaction is involvement in the crimes of society, that the responsibility of a corporate body such as a professional group is no different from the responsibility of an individual: to act with a conscience. The effort to transform the professional associations is a bit like the work of community organizations to which the Left has committed itself. This kind of radicalism may have a less dramatic career than other varieties, but possibly one with a firmer effect.

The agitation against the university for its traffic with the governmental establishment made a clear argument. The pressure for curricular reform represents something more subtle, and often misunderstood. The idea many people appear to have gotten is one of a radical student who insists that the courses, from ancient archeology to twentieth-century art, be politicized, and that he be given the privilege of hearing, through one class after another, a recital of his own Left ideology. Undoubtedly there are students who have demanded such a curriculum, and who could go through a semester or two of it without crumbling with boredom. But others ask for a curriculum that prepares them sensitively and flexibly in the techniques of achieving social justice. And a notable variety is the student, quite thoroughly radicalized in his politics, who rejects the standard curriculum because it is not intellectual and imaginative enough, allows no experimentation in forms (say, a collage in place of a term paper), and is too stiffly serviceable to the business of getting through school and getting a job—too "relevant," if you will. Even here there is a political implication of sorts. A curriculum aiming at the encouragement of a rich sensibility could be a beginning for the elevation of consciousness that the cultural radicals seek also in political change.

In sum, many of the student radicals have been willing, consciously or implicitly, to complicate experience by conjoining it to processes and techniques. The civil rights movement early in the sixties represented a passion controlled by strategy and by personal restraint. The two marches on Washington in the autumn of 1969 were experiential and communal, but they were so partly because they were well organized and because their participants had some instinct of courtesy. These are interesting mixtures, and they suggest by analogy what a good university life might be also: a fluent commerce between intuition and intellectual discipline.

The movement for black awareness is not usually identified with the counterculture. But it gets to some of the same points: communalism, identity, and the reconstitution of experience. And the supposition on which it acts—that the black man, who does not possess the identity America bestows on the white, can find an identity only by founding himself in the collective experience of his own people—has both a strength and a perilousness to it that recalls the delicate balance of tendencies within the rest of radicalism. Folk, place, nation—all these do give identity; they also destroy it, deny to the individual his privacy of taste or intention, and swallow up his will. To preserve personal independence and integrity requires careful strategies of dipping into a cultural situation as well as disengagement from it.

The courageous black youths of the civil rights movement had been from the classes most assimilated to white America: college students, young members of the middle class, and what many civil rights workers described as the "striving lower classes." And their cause, even when their style had to be that of a radical remnant, was essentially assimilationist. But events were to take another direction. The movement taught all black people, in and out of it, to define problems in racial terms, and when, after Birmingham, the ghetto streets no longer were silent witnesses of the spectacle, the younger and more radical leaders turned from white liberals to the black poor in search of their allies and potential source of power, transforming the middle-class integration movement into the radical black power movement.

The slogan "Black Power" was apparently first coined by Adam Clayton Powell in his commencement address at Howard University in 1966, but it became nationally famous—notorious, in fact—when Stokely Carmichael immediately picked it up as a chant during the march through Mississippi that James Meredith led in June 1966. Coming after two summers of rioting and the promise of more, it received wide press play as a new departure in the black movement. The hysterical response to it throughout the nation ensured that it would be just that. Carmichael had discovered how to use the angers released and heightened by the ghetto rioting to undercut the established civil rights leadership. The new rhetoric stressed black independence and political power in place of integration with whites, emphasized community development over individual advancement, and called for meeting violence with violence rather than passive resistance. It insisted upon the title "black," in place of the "Negro" that had once been itself a victory. The white man's exaggeration of the African color, which identified it linguistically with soot, evil, and all negation, was now virtue. "Black is beautiful." Blacks ceased processing their hair and bleaching their skin. Soul food became a cuisine instead of a necessity; soul music expressed ethnic distinctness more deliberately than had the older, and perhaps more

African, Afro-American rhythms and tones; black theater companies came on the stage to explore the riches of the black experience; artists worked strong motifs in stark splashes of color.

Many things account for this. The obvious sources were the new political power of the ghetto, the social and economic gains, the pride that came first with the civil rights movement and then with its successors. But more elusive factors were at work. One was the rise of black Africa. Another was the uses the white counterculture was finding for black modes of expression. The music of that culture borrowed first from jazz, among the beats, then from Negro rhythm and blues, and finally from the older blues traditions. The hipster style drew upon the ghetto zootsuiter. Encounters with the police and the prisons were a large subject in the blues traditions, and whites in alienation or revolt found there a ready source of attitudes and wisdom. The radical political element in the youth culture turned to the black community as a possible ground from which to attack the status quo. Its feeling and tempo added something to the imagination of the counterculture.

A fairly quiet instance of the revolution in consciousness has taken place within the churches, among a portion of the ministry, priest-hood, and laity. It is one of the many returns that Christianity makes to its sources; more specifically, it is a response in particular to two events, the civil rights movement and the liturgical experi-mentation that was especially if indirectly the result of the liberaliza-tion within the Roman Catholic Church undertaken at the Second Vatican Council of 1962–1965, "Vatican II." Within the rights move-ment, the Christian Left discovered evangelical community; through the liturgies of the folk mass predominantly, but also of the jazz and the rock mass, it gained a renewed feeling for the Eucharist. Eucharist and the community of protest have together defined a new—or rather, an ancient—Christianity.

Liberal Protestants as well as liberal Catholics have taken to the experimental liturgies. Some of these are of a considerable beauty, but since Christianity has at its disposal a great music and liturgy, much of the attractiveness the new kinds possess is for special reasons: a fresh simplicity that the music conveys, and the intimacy of the services. In lessening the distance between the sacrament and the communicant, and in drawing the congregation together into an informal gathering where the worshiper shares with his fellows the songs and the ceremony rather than resting passive and isolated, the new mass has had the effect of giving esthetic expression to one central meaning of the Eucharistic sacrament— that whether it is received publicly or by a handful, it is for the recipients, in their moment of communion with Christ, a moment also of community with one another. It has other theological meanings, and liturgical details to lend them form; but the new mass has recalled Christianity, or liberal Christians, to this significance of it. The enactment of the experimental liturgy has therefore a social bearing as well, for it can be the perfect statement of the quest for a community redeemed of racial division and made regenerate.

Meanwhile, churchmen were participating in the civil rights movement, and there were finding community in another of its characters. In the South, the activism got much of its quality from the black Protestant churches, and the congregational and evangelical spirit that they brought to it was reinforced by the strategies of the sit-in and the comradeship of effort and peril. The new Christianity is to be found at the intersection of these communal imperatives: the rights movement gave substance to community and the Eucharistic liturgy gave it clear articulation.

This Christian Left has drawn in other ways from its era. The measures of liberalization taken at Vatican II, and the quickening of experience that came of the new liturgies, have made it vibrant; the sense of immediacy between the sacrament and the recipient, the sacrament and the community of worshipers, has strengthened the idea that all life is sacramental: "celebrate life," the new Christians urge in their worship and their banners. A gentle experiential feeling infuses the new Christianity, a responsiveness to inner experience and to the sacramental presence in the details of existence; but here, as with the rest of the cultural Left, is the risk. Despite some important theology, this celebrative Christianity can often be impatient of precise formulation; it has lost a bit of the tough skepticism about human nature that traditional Christianity possesses with the conception of original sin; and its experiential mood, which on the one hand can sharpen into exactness and differentiation of experience, threatens on the other to lapse into sentiment.

The new Christianity has another side to it, a prophetic conscience formed by the racial and social issues of the sixties. That conscience, possibly one the finest things that will be remembered of the period, has sent priests and ministers into the ghettos, created projects of social action, and called up acts of witness and protest such as the invasion of draft centers by priests and nuns. It has a good deal in common with the milder kind of Left Christianity, for its bent is not toward close theological statement but toward direct experiential encounter with fact and with the sacramental moral command that may lie there. And again, there is a precarious balance between tendencies; for the conscience of the Christian Left has within it, like all conscience but with particular force, an impulse to arrogance and stridency that may betray it at every step.

Many movements on the new cultural Left have brought experiential radicalism into some sort of relationship with the larger political and social world. The Left is known also for two phenomena that appear to be almost exclusively experiential, and the private possession of the underground. Drugs and progressive rock are subject, like all the other activities the public associates with the counterculture, to being made into stereotypes and shows. Both of them offer alterations of experience and may therefore reach significantly into the mind of the new Left. But the drug user submits, however willingly, to the recasting, while the rock performer controls it.

One of the great American drug scenes has been in the middle class, which in the 1950s was heavily consuming tranquilizers for nervousness and amphetamines for overweight. The most common drug in the radical culture is marijuana. It comes from the tops of a common plant that grows widely and in many varieties. In earlier times it was a standard American patent medicine. As a stimulant, however, it has a shorter past in this country. Mexican immigrants introduced marijuana smoking into Texas and California early in this century, and it quickly took hold among New Orleans jazz musicians. From there it spread with the black migrations and became an underground drug, passing within groups considered beyond the pale of respectability, such as jazz musicians, criminals, delinquents, prostitutes, and homosexuals. The beats in the fifties picked up the habit from the jazz musicians. Since 1962 the use of drugs has risen sharply on the college campuses.

Marijuana is the mildest of the so-called head drugs, drugs the primary effect of which is on the psychic state rather than on physiological feeling. The distinction, while not precise or definitive, does broadly differentiate the tendency of hallucinogenic drugs such as marijuana, peyote, and the synthetics such as LSD, mescaline, and STP from that of the various stimulants and depressants: amphetamines, alcohol, barbiturates, and narcotics. Stronger head drugs have a long history in various religious traditions. The first of these to reach American culture was peyote, used in certain Mexican Indian cults; and mescaline, the active ingredient in peyote, could be chemically synthesized. Gary Snyder, a beat poet who remains an important figure in the hippie bohemia, learned of peyote from Mexican Indians, and introduced it to the beats in the early fifties; it was the source of the phantasmagorical Mexican trip at the end of Kerouac's *On the Road*. In 1957 and 1958 peyote and mescaline were the rage in New York's Greenwich Village. But soon a more powerful and easily procurable synthetic hallucinogen, LSD, became available. LSD (Lysergic Acid Diethylamide, hence "acid") was synthesized in 1938 as an intermediate compound in the synthesis of other chemicals. The first man known to take an acid trip was Dr. Albert Hoffman, one of the original synthesizers, who, on April 16, 1943, accidentally absorbed enough of the chemical to experience two hours of "a peculiar state similar to drunkenness, characterized by an exaggerated imagination." LSD began its progress through the American cultural underworld from Greenwich Village, where LSD began arriving in quantity in the winter of 1961–1962. Before that, it had apparently been restricted generally to medical personnel and researchers such as Timothy Leary, then in the psychology department at Harvard. By 1964 it had arrived in the San Francisco area, and two years later Ken Kesey had spread the gospel far beyond the confines of bohemia with the "acid tests," rock performances with stoned crowds. After Kesey's exploits, the drug began to hit the colleges, and scattered sociological reports indicate that in the later 1960s the number of users spread with a rapidity more or less duplicating the spread of marijuana earlier in the decade; by 1970, however, its use had declined. Timothy Leary, the high priest of acid since he was fired from the psychology department at Harvard, made a contribution to the drug's spread perhaps equal to Kesey's when in 1964 he published the recipe for synthesizing the chemical— a process that appeared to be quite simple, until people discovered how easy it was to make a bad batch of LSD. But it is a distrusted drug; it has an extraordinary power to induce what some have called "transient psychoses," and it can bring the nightmare of a bad trip.

Some experimented with even more powerful hallucinogens such as STP, while others turned to massive dosages of amphetamines— "Speed"—to go for days without sleep into exhaustion-induced Nirvanas or joyless bouts of psychotic violence. "Speed kills" was the word in the underground, and "speed freaks" became the madmen of a mad land, distrusted even by the drug culture.

The cultural effects of the drugs seem to be various. In some ways they may be communal. The ritual of marijuana smoking among a group has a communal air, and the drowsy relaxation of the will and senses may perhaps do something toward making of the smokers a community. Yet it can just as easily limit positive communion and exchange, and let the user fall back into the private experience the drug has effected within him. LSD throws the individual into a temporary personal universe; and some drugs can cause hostility.

Progressive rock and its immediate predecessors have drawn upon a wide heritage of folk, blues, and country music. Hard rock has attained a curious fusion of opposites: on materials chosen specifically for their folkish quality, it has imposed strange and sophisticated techniques, and in particular, the modern technology of electrical amplification and tone. Twentieth-century technology, in fact, had already given of itself to the old musics before progressive rock took them up.

The preservation of folk music has been accomplished by the methods of scholarship and the means of recording that an urban technological society provides. The folk revival of the late fifties and early sixties depended upon earlier work on the part of ethnomusicologists, who had studiously gathered and set down the old songs. A Victorian Englishman, Cecil Sharp, collected ballads in America during World War I. Charles Seeger, Pete's father and an academic ethnomusicologist, and John A. and Alan Lomax employed the new technology of recording as they traveled through the various isolated areas of the South and West collecting versions of songs, now on precious tapes at the Library of Congress. At first this effort at preservation did not aim to make the music popular, since popularizing was considered to be a species of destruction; and folk music in the forties and fifties remained largely a preserve of the small American Left, which had discovered the music in its rejection of bourgeois values and its attempts to organize the dispossessed. Toward the end of the fifties, however, a folk revival appeared, centered in New York City's Greenwich Village. It started by being heavily derivative, carefully following the old tapes and the versions that Sharp had presented in his great *English Folk Songs from the Southern Appalachians*. Bob Dylan sounded enough like the legendary balladeer Woody Guthrie, dying of Huntington's chorea in Graystone Hospital, to startle many of his early listeners. But pedantry had its uses for revolution. The urban musicians and composers began to create folk ballads as had Guthrie and the great blues artist Leadbelly, and folk proved peculiarly forceful for political statement. As a music of the people, the poor and hidden of the past, it caught the imagination of the Left; many of its tones seemed a distant call from naive and pastoral ages innocent of the technological corruptions many of its devotees were learning to dread; and its pure clear notes, with their peculiar directness and appeal, carried the messages with much effect. Some of the original songs, moreover, had been of protest; and these conveyed their listeners back over the dormant fifties to World War II, the early labor movement, and the Great Depression. The old songs and the new ones were to sound the dominant chord of the radicalism that was emerging, an amalgam of pacifism, radical politics, and a nostalgia for innocence—a blend almost undefinable within the conventional terms of the conflict between Left and Right.

Folk found its way into folk rock, and then became an element in hard rock, which also incorporated Negro blues and white country music. Though these two had their origins in preindustrial cultures, they had evolved into their later forms partly through a considerable working association with modern technology. Radio and the record industry had allowed for considerable decentralization. Programs like "Grand Ole Opry," beginning in 1925 and emanating from a Nashville radio station, both preserved and transformed country music, removing it from a strictly oral tradition, opening the possibilities of new instrumentation and cross-fertilizing from other styles, yet keeping it among a sufficiently limited audience to retain its country flavor. The blues had a similar history: artists like Muddy Waters adopted such innovations as the electric guitar, while the music was confined mostly to black clubs and radio stations.

Each of these three musical traditions, folk, blues, and country, reached back beyond industrial times, but each had some involvements with electronic technology. Progressive rock introduced them to further technical advance—acoustical augmentation, especially through the eight-track recording machine, and elaborate electronic processing of what the musician had originally put on his tapes. At times these techniques have added much complexity to the labor and the result. "Sgt. Pepper's Lonely Hearts Club Band," the Beatles' masterpiece, took nine hundred hours of studio time to record. The culture that this splendid medley represented was itself a medley. That remarkable record jacket, with the Beatles in band uniform and backed by a throng of famous figures, the Beatles again among them in different guise, suggests a person who will not be pinned down to a single identity, who will try in turn, or if possible simultaneously, every attractive identity. He will be all the heroes of his own movie. The Beatles were not settling into any success rut, cautiously duplicating their last record. The rumor, given international currency, of Paul McCartney's death was symbolic. The Beatles were burying old styles for new ones; they would be reborn at every chance they got.

Like much of the musical tradition it incorporates, rock is communal. In a rock festival such as Woodstock, the audience participates in the event and completes it—not by joining in with the music in any major way, but by forming with one another and with the artists a community of experience and will. If the concert is indoors, the hall will cease to be the typical neutral room where classical music has been played the night before and a "packaged" wedding party will take place the day after; set with lights and equipment and filled with an audience flamboyantly garbed, it will be—even if rented only for the evening—a full environment of music, people, and surroundings. The flashings of colors, distinct but belonging to the whole, from the clothes of the audience and from the lights are like the flash of parts in the music; the individuality among the listeners is like that of each player, whose contribution, however precise and subordinate to the total work it may actually be, sometimes appears to cooperate with that of his fellow performers more by a sort of alliance or confluence than by an absolutely controlling design: in this, rock resembles jazz. It is an invocation to community; it is also a testing at the fringes of consciousness, and a play among the disparate elements of awareness—sounds that are mystic and distant, others robustly earthbound, rough patternings and flowing tones.

In one of its forms, the new culture is present in a special type of society that already by 1967 was in a state of permanent siege, surrounded by the media and a prey to all the pathologies of the cities in which it centered, especially the East Village in New York and the Haight-Ashbury section of San Francisco. By that time the flowers and gentleness, the drugs and generosity and confusion, had produced gruesome incidents and were on their way to becoming a cliché of the mass media. This society—not at all synonymous with communes, which are of many kinds—is best described by the negations it makes. It rejects bureaucracy and insists on personal relationships. It may reject rationality along with hierarchy: the lowly and the insane are welcome. It scorns material gains. It turns from jobs: machines will do all the dull labor. It rejects certain middle-class notions, especially privacy and accepted styles of dress. It rejects hypocrisy about sex, and with it some of the secretiveness that middle-class people demand. There has been an attempt to eliminate sharp differentiation in sexual manner, with boys and girls dressing alike and wearing their hair at similar length.

This gentle fringe of dissidents represents differing objectives; among these may be a desire to keep the possibilities of identity open, to blur outlines of the self that would fasten the individual to a single future, blur them with the use of drugs and through submission to collective experience. The denial of definiteness implies a denial of power. Power means the impress of yourself on the world, and to keep your identity fluid you must avoid making that impress, avoid creating a structure of expectations among those around you that then fixes your actions and finally your character. Even violence can fix self-identity. In violence, Frantz Fanon has observed, the person has no choice but to define himself—though we might except from this the violence that is the collapse of mind and will into pure emotion.

For those radicals who have turned to power, Herbert Marcuse, a philosopher of the Left, has supplied a post-Marxist critique of the twentieth century, and demonstrated how Marxism can be a supple and growing thing. The conception of the working class as antithesis to capitalism, argues Marcuse, will no longer do; by prosperity and by psychological conditioning capitalist society has absorbed the established labor class into its false consciousness, while the particular kind of tolerance it practices sends a mist over the clear contours of opposition and argument. Dialectic is flattened into consensus. The true dialectic, Marcuse believes, must occur in the imagination rather than in economics merely. Marcuse looks to the cultural Left for dialectical sensibility that can project a radical alternative to the capitalist consciousness. This sensibility will restore the hard precision of language, which capitalist propaganda has rendered limp. It will liberate for control over the technological process the playful energies that capitalism has stiffened; it will perceive forms of reality outside the terms in which a capitalist people thinks.

There is a dialectic that schools the imagination to a high order of rigor and vividness; it is a habit of looking for contrasts even in small details, a defining of facts by their opposites, and an analysis of things by the contradictions within them, and under its scrutiny existence becomes alive with tension and variegation. That is a lesson some of the radicals could learn from Marcuse. Or they could hold only to the simplest understanding of his categories: then capitalist society would appear to them a monolith, totally false in its consciousness and unacceptable in any of its efforts; and against it they would be tempted to oppose an equally monolithic consciousness in rebellion, undiscriminating in intellect or in sensitivity. This state Marcuse would not wish of radicalism, but it is the easier and possibly the more predictable course.

epilogue

Social scientists have discovered in American political history a recurrent cycle of political coalitions, emerging in the 1790s, 1820s, 1850s, and 1930s, in which a stable coalition politics dissolves, then composes itself into a new coalition, correspondent to new issues, that maintains the political peace for another generation. All of these changes in American politics have had their violent side. The 1790s ended with threats of civil war (Virginia actually bought arms), the election of 1828 seemed a revolution, the 1850s were a time of great violence and their issues were resolved in war, the nineties brought Coxey's Army, bloody strikes, and fears of social revolution and anarchy. The angers of the 1930s remain part of our memory and folklore.

At first glance the 1960s appeared to be of a like political nature. It had seemed as early as 1958 that a period of fluctuation on the order of earlier ones was upon us. Perhaps a liberal coalition was forming, or possibly in a new era of policy and debate a liberal collapse would lead to a conservative politics. Instead the 1960 election, with its curious cross-pressuring from the religious issue, fell back into the politics of stalemate that had overtaken the New Deal coalition in the forties, a stalemate based upon a conservative leadership in Congress and a continuing alternation of the presidency among candidates frozen by their slender majorities into executive inaction. Then the death of Kennedy, Johnson's accession, and Goldwater's failure in 1964 seemed to settle American politics into a liberal course. Even before Johnson's reelection, however, his response to the Tonkin Gulf incident began a process that would prevent his solidifying the country around a new enduring liberal coalition in the spiritual lineage of the New Deal. In 1968 the Democratic party was driven from the presidency and a moderate Republican returned by a small margin. Nixon's attempt to rally a new conservative coalition has been unsuccessful. A Republican President faces a Democratic Congress, and both parties had already made their bid for a new politics and failed. In sum, the political fluctuation that America had entered in the late Eisenhower years still continues into the seventies. We have neither a stable politics of division between the parties as in the late nineteenth century, nor a practical dominance by either party; nor have the new and ill-defined issues that had hovered at the edges of political debate managed to take full control, displacing the economic questions that had occupied American public discourse since the New Deal. Commentators talk of a "social issue"—crime, public order, the quality of life, the role of youth, even the basis of personality and community—but politicians aided by the most careful analyses of public opinion are unable to find the tone that will reach the anxieties of the nation. The "New Politics" of 1968 was liberal and left; the "New Politics" of 1970 was right: neither has succeeded.

The older pattern, in which coalitions periodically form to renovate American political life, has not repeated itself. That pattern required distinct symbolic issues that could be flatly decided in a single direction: the extension of slavery, the free coinage of silver, the national responsibility for welfare—questions that lend themselves to the simple answer that a vote can register, and that gather interests and political groups into distinct opposing camps. In 1860, 1896, and 1936, the meaning of the vote was particularly clear. Such decisions are no longer possible in American politics. Prior commitments, the complex lasting responsibilities of government, preclude them. Whatever kind of referendum the election of 1964 might have been was vitiated from the start: on Johnson's election he was forced into a belligerent foreign policy by the logic of established commitments; had Goldwater been elected, the larger part of his domestic politics would have been predetermined by the structures of government, especially by its concrete obligations to manage the national economy. "We are all Keynesians now," said his chief economic adviser, and we were all interventionists as well.

The language of politics has for a time become meaningless or confusing, and more and more people are directing their political energies to conflicts outside of formal politics. Rock concerts and estivals have turned into quasi-political events, struggles for power between youth and local people. A Fourth of July celebration became in 1970, with semiofficial backing, a statement of an older culture against the new. Comedians have discovered that their humor is conservative—or liberal. In the colleges, avant-garde students deny the possibility of divorcing intellectual activity from politics. Political institutions seem relatively helpless to draw to themselves major social forces, which instead spill broadly over society—perhaps dissipating themselves, perhaps working creatively.

The sixties have had their special pungencies of style. John F. Kennedy tried to cast the world in the form of a moral drama. Norman Mailer, who caught one spirit of the decade sooner than almost any other writer, believed that heroism of a cool new kind would be the temper. Martin Luther King brought to his times a distinctive manner: never has heroism been so precise, never have confrontations in America been so carefully defined, so chivalrous in their intentions, so aristocratic in their mixture of boldness and restraint. Old intellectual and cultural forms have been broken. The Cold War psychology worked itself out to a terrible denouement and lost its hold. A long tradition of liberalism reached its end in a liberal state that could no longer distinguish itself from the forces it had once tried to control, and in a liberal community that in ceasing to serve only as a national conscience would struggle to develop its own private ethos. Young people have moved from the interstices of American institutions into a measure of power. The fragmentation that has marked American life for some time has found its own counterforce in the consolidation of subcultures, each with its own voice and view, in a way that has enriched America even while it has complicated our politics.

bibliography

I. Eisenhower's Second Administration

No extensive scholarly attention has been paid to the second Eisenhower administration. Two of the President's speech writers have written good books that treat the later Eisenhower: Emmet John Hughes, *The Ordeal of Power* (1963), and Arthur Larson, *Eisenhower: The President Nobody Knew* (1968). Excellent brief essays on Eisenhower are Richard Rovere, "Eisenhower over the Shoulder," *American Scholar* (1961), and Murray Kempton, "The Underestimation of Dwight Eisenhower," *Esquire* (1967); see also the collection of articles edited by Dean Albertson, *Eisenhower As President* (1963). Eisenhower's own memoirs, *The White House Years: Waging Peace, 1956–1961* (1965), are not especially inclusive. Two important sets of documents are *Goals for Americans: The Report of the President's Commission on National Goals* (1960) and *Peace with Justice: Selected Addresses of Dwight D. Eisenhower* (1961).

An enormously useful chronicle and analysis of legislative history for the 1950s and 1960s is James L. Sundquist, *Politics and Policy: The Eisenhower, Kennedy, and Johnson Years* (1968). For a clarification of the Eisenhower electoral appeal see Agnus Campbell et al., *The American Voter* (1960), and Samuel Lubell, *The Revolt of the Moderates* (1956). Eisenhower's perennial Democratic opponent is the subject of two recent books: Bert Cochran, *Adlai Stevenson: Patrician among the Politicians* (1969), and Herbert J. Muller, *Adlai Stevenson* (1968). The foreign policy of John Foster Dulles is the subject of *Duel at the Brink* (1960) by Roscoe Drummond and Gaston Coblentz; the secretary's own statements are edited by Andrew H. Berding, *Dulles on Diplomacy* (1965).

II. Social Criticism

David Riesman, Reuel Denney, and Nathan Glazer, *The Lonely Crowd* (1950), captures beyond any other single work the way intellectuals in the 1950s learned to conceive of America. See also Riesman's *Faces in the Crowd* (1952) and *Individualism Reconsidered* (1954). C. Wright Mills, *White Collar* (1953) and *The Power Elite* (1956), are works of social analysis whose impact has not yet been spent. The same can be said of John Kenneth Galbraith, *American Capitalism* (1956) and *The Affluent Society* (1958), and Michael Harrington, *The Other America* (1962). Daniel Bell, ed., *The New American Right* (1955), well illustrates the intellectual mood of the fifties, which has been criticized in detail by Michael Rogin in *The Intellectuals and McCarthy* (1967). See also Bell's influential *The End of Ideology* (1960). Grant McConnell, *Private Power and American Democracy* (1966), and Theodore J. Lowi, *The End of Liberalism* (1969), are major critiques of the body of social thought culminating during the early sixties. Lawrence Lipton, *The Holy Barbarians* (1959), is still the best book on the beats. Jack Kerouac, *On the Road* (1957), and Allen Ginsberg, *Howl, and Other Poems* (1956), give the flavor of the movement. On Ginsberg see Jane Kramer, *Allen Ginsberg in America* (1969). The early years of the *Evergreen Review* are rich in beat writings.

Of the large literature on youth and education, the works of James S. Coleman are of great value. *The Adolescent Society* (1961) and *Adolescents and the Schools* (1965) provide hard data and sharp insight. Paul Goodman's *Growing Up Absurd* (1960) has had a wide influence. His *The Empire City* (1959) is a brilliant novel depicting the problems of growing up in the era, which is also the concern of J. D. Salinger's *The Catcher in the Rye* (1951), about a sensitive adolescent. See also the works of Edgar Z. Friedenberg, especially *The Vanishing Adolescent* (1959), which is prophetic in its recognition of the tensions developing between generations in the era. James A. Wechsler, *Reflections of an Angry Middle-Aged Editor* (1960), is perceptive on the cultural changes taking place late in the decade and their effect on differing generations.

Writings on suburbia extend through the fifties and sixties. William H. Whyte, *The Organization Man* (1956), influenced many views of the new Americans beyond the city. John R. Seeley, *Crestwood Heights* (1956), and Robert C. Wood, *Suburbia, Its People and Their Politics* (1959), are solid sociological studies. Marshall Sklare and Joseph Greenblum, *Jewish Identity on the Suburban Frontier* (1967), and Herbert J. Gans, *The Levittowners* (1967), carry these themes into the sixties. Scott Donaldson, *The Suburban Myth* (1969), examines views of the suburbs.

III. John F. Kennedy

Arthur Schlesinger's *A Thousand Days* (1965) is a monument to the Kennedy era, giving shape to the period by its very inclusiveness, especially on the making of foreign policy. A similar work by the President's long-term adviser, Theodore C. Sorenson, *Kennedy* (1965), is useful but has a more limited perspective. Victor Lasky lets loose an often irrational attack in *JFK: The Man and the Myth* (1963). See also Tom Wicker, *Kennedy without Tears: The Man behind the Myth* (1964). Aida DiPace Donald has edited a group of important articles: *John F. Kennedy and the New Frontier* (1966). See also William G. Carleton, "Kennedy in History: An Early Appraisal," *Antioch Review* (1964), and George Kateb, "Kennedy As Statesman," *Commentary* (1966).

The 1960 campaign and election are covered in Eric Sevareid, ed., *Candidates 1960* (1959); Theodore White, *The Making of the President 1960* (1961); Paul T. David et al., *The Presidential Election and Transition 1960– 1961* (1961); Philip Converse et al., "Stability and Change in 1960: A Reinstating Election," *American Political Science Review* (1961); Sidney Kraus, ed., *The Great Debates* (1962); and in Norman Mailer's acute portrait of Kennedy as he stirred the subconscious, reprinted in Mailer's *The Presidential Papers of Nor-*

man Mailer (1964). The Big Steel episode of 1962 is treated by Grant McConnell, *Steel and the Presidency —1962* (1963). The congressional deadlock of 1962–1963 is examined in James MacGregor Burns, *The Deadlock of Democracy* (1963). The last chapter of Robert Lekachman's *Age of Keynes* (1966) is good on the economy under Kennedy and Johnson. On the Supreme Court see Alexander Bickel, *The Supreme Court and the Idea of Progress* (1970). Monographs on the Kennedy administration have already begun to appear: Jim F. Heath, *John F. Kennedy and the Business Community* (1969), and Lawrence H. Fuchs, *John F. Kennedy and American Catholicism* (1967).

Dean Rusk's statements in an important period have been edited by Ernest K. Lindley, *The Winds of Freedom: Selections from Speeches and Statements of Secretary of State Dean Rusk, January 1961–August 1962* (1963). Maxwell Taylor's works are essential for an understanding of the period, particularly *An Uncertain Trumpet* (1960) and *Responsibility and Response* (1967).

Works on Kennedy's assassination abound—and still they come. See, for example, Thomas G. Buchanan, *Who Killed Kennedy?* (1964); Leo Sauvage, *The Oswald Affair* (1966); Josiah Thompson, *Six Seconds in Dallas* (1967); William Manchester, *The Death of a President* (1967); Sylvia Meagher, *Accessories after the Fact: The Warren Commission, the Authorities and the Report* (1967); Mark Lane, *A Citizen's Dissent* (1968); and Edward Jay Epstein, *Counterplot* (1969). A handbook of selections from the Warren report has been published by McGraw-Hill and the *New York Times* as *The Witnesses* (1965).

IV. The Civil Rights Movement and Black Power

The black man's struggle in the sixties has created an enormous literature. James Baldwin was perhaps the most successful black writer at evoking the mood of the early sixties. See his *Notes of a Native Son* (1957), *Nobody Knows My Name* (1961), and *The Fire Next Time* (1963). Martin Luther King, Jr., is best approached through his own writings: *Stride toward* also the critical biography by John A. Williams, *The Freedom* (1958) and *Why We Can't Wait* (1964); see *King God Didn't Save* (1970). Other memoirs and writings of participants are the classic *The Autobiography of Malcolm X* (1965), Claude Brown, *Manchild in the*

Promised Land (1965), and Eldridge Cleaver, *Soul on Ice* (1967). H. R. Isaacs, *The New World of Negro Americans* (1963), is important on the meaning of emerging Africa. Charles Silberman, *Crisis in Black and White* (1964), is an honest and thoughtful book. Leonard Broom and Norval Glenn, *Transformation of the Negro American* (1965), is a valuable sociological study. Howard Zinn, *SNCC: The New Abolitionists* (1964), and Jack Newfield, *A Prophetic Minority* (1966), are useful on SNCC.

Several important books have studied public opinion on race. Samuel Lubell, *White and Black: Test of a Nation* (1964), and William Brink and Louis Harris, *Black and White: A Study of U.S. Racial Attitudes Today* (1967), are both useful, as is Lubell's later *The Hidden Crisis in American Politics* (1970), which is not exclusively about race. Robert Coles, *Children of Crisis* (1967), is a perceptive account of the human meaning of desegregation.

Harold Cruse, *The Crisis of the Negro Intellectual* (1967), and *Rebellion or Revolution?* (1968), offer special insights into the intellectual traditions out of which the ideology of black power emerges. Theodore Draper, *The Rediscovery of Black Nationalism* (1970), is also illuminating on this subject. Charles V. Hamilton and Stokely Carmichael state their case in *Black Power* (1967). Kenneth Clark, *Dark Ghetto* (1965), offers solid insights into the society of the black ghetto. Chuck Stone, *Black Political Power in America* (1968), is useful on black political assertion. Ulf Hannerz, *Soulside* (1969), is a valuable anthropological study of life in a Washington ghetto. Daniel P. Moynihan and Nathan Glazer, *Beyond the Melting Pot* (1963), contains a discussion of ghetto life, as does the highly controversial "Moynihan Report," which is best read in Lee Rainwater and William Yancey, *The Moynihan Report and the Politics of Controversy* (1967). Charles Keil, *Urban Blues* (1966), combines musicology, cultural anthropology, social history, and acute sensitivity to create a classic study illuminating the mind of the urban ghetto. Lewis M. Killian, *The Impossible Revolution: Black Power and the American Dream* (1968), presents a penetrating argument and a chilling perspective.

V. *Lyndon B. Johnson*

There is a large biography of President Johnson, *Sam Johnson's Boy* (1968), by Alfred Steinberg. The best books on Johnson, however, are shorter ones, including

Tom Wicker, *JFK and LBJ: The Influence of Personality upon Politics* (1968), Michael Davie, *LBJ: A Foreign Observer's Viewpoint* (1966), and Hugh Sidey, *A Very Personal Presidency: Lyndon Johnson in the White House* (1968). Other books on Johnson include Eric Goldman, *The Tragedy of Lyndon Johnson* (1969); Rowland Evans and Robert Novak, *Lyndon B. Johnson: The Exercise of Power* (1966); Jack Bell, *The Johnson Treatment: How Lyndon B. Johnson Took Over the Presidency and Made It His Own* (1965); William S. White, *The Professional: Lyndon B. Johnson* (1964); Philip Geyelin, *Lyndon B. Johnson and the World* (1966); and Leonard Baker, *The Johnson Eclipse* (1966). Johnson's speeches and messages are handily collected by Atheneum publishers in *A Time for Action: A Selection from the Speeches and Writings of Lyndon B. Johnson, 1953–1964* (1964), and James MacGregor Burns, ed., *To Heal and to Build: The Programs of President Lyndon B. Johnson* (1968). The latter, incidentally, contains Ralph Ellison's "The Myth of the Flamed White Southerner." On the 1964 election there are Walter Dean Burnham, "American Voting Behavior and the 1964 Election," *Midwest Journal of Political Science* (1966); Milton C. Cummings, ed., *The National Election of 1964* (1966); and Theodore White, *The Making of the President 1964* (1965). Angus Campbell et al., *Elections and the Political Order* (1966), touches on the political fluctuations of the era. On Goldwater see the essay in Richard Hofstadter, *The Paranoid Style in American Politics* (1965); Richard Rovere, *The Goldwater Caper* (1965); Stephen Shadegg, *What Happened to Goldwater?* (1965); and Clifton White, *Suite 3505: The Story of the Draft Goldwater Movement* (1967). Goldwater's own books are *The Conscience of a Conservative* (1960), *Why Not Victory* (1962), *Where I Stand* (1964), and *Conscience of a Majority* (1970).

Walter Heller, chairman of the Council of Economic Advisers, published *New Dimensions of Political Economy* (1966). James Sundquist's *Politics and Policy: The Eisenhower, Kennedy, and Johnson Years* is especially valuable for its coverage of Great Society legislation. A defense of our role in the Dominican Republic has been written by John B. Martin, our ambassador there under Kennedy, *Overtaken by Events* (1966).

VI. Vietnam

Historical accounts on Vietnam include the standard George M. Kahin and John W. Lewis, *The United States in Vietnam* (1967); Chester A. Bain, *Vietnam: The Roots of Conflict* (1967); John T. McAlister, Jr., *Vietnam: The Origins of Revolution* (1969); the two-volume Joseph Buttinger, *Vietnam: A Dragon Embattled* (1967); Philippe Devillers and Jean Lacouture, *End of a War: Indochina, 1954* (rev. 1969); and Melvin Gurtov, *The First Vietnam Crisis: Chinese Communist Strategy and United States Involvement 1953–1954* (1967). Perhaps a good pair of introductions to American intervention are Ralph K. White, *Nobody Wanted War* (1968), and the more critical Henry Brandon, *Anatomy of Error: The Inside Story of the Asian War on the Potomac, 1954–1969* (1969). See also the recent "inside" accounts: Chester L. Cooper, *The Lost Crusade* (1970), and Townsend Hoopes, *The Limits of Intervention* (1969). Journalists have been among the first critics of the war, and one of the finest was Bernard B. Fall, killed in Vietnam in 1967 by a mine explosion. His books include *Street without Joy: Insurgency in Indo-China, 1946–1963* (1963), *The Two Viet-Nams: A Political and Military Analysis* (1967), *Last Reflections on a War* (1967), and *Anatomy of a Crisis: The Laos Crisis of Nineteen Sixty-One* (1969).

Critical accounts abound. They include Theodore Draper, *Abuse of Power* (1967); Arthur M. Schlesinger, Jr., *The Bitter Heritage: Vietnam and American Democracy, 1941–1966* (1967); Noam Chomsky, *American Power and the New Mandarins* (1969), which seeks to destroy the "myth" of objectivity and liberal scholarship, and his *At War with Asia* (1970); Jean-Paul Sartre, *On Genocide* (1968); Mary McCarthy, *Vietnam* (1967) and *Hanoi* (1968); Howard Zinn, *Vietnam: The Logic of Withdrawal* (1967); Staughton Lynd and Thomas Hayden, *The Other Side* (1966); Harry S. Ashmore and William C. Baggs, *Mission to Hanoi* (1968); Bertrand Russell, *War Crimes in Vietnam* (1967); Seymour Melman, *Pentagon Capitalism* (1970); and Hans Morgenthau, *Truth and Power* (1970). An extremely important critique, although not perhaps for its indictment of American imperialism, is Carl Oglesby's "Essay on the Meaning of the Cold War," which appeared in Carl Oglesby and Richard Shaull, *Containment and Change* (1967). Richard M. Pfeffer, ed., *No More Vietnams: The War and the Future of American Foreign Policy* (1968), is an excellent collection of opinions.

Since the United States Senate encouraged debate on the war, it is appropriate that individual senators should have written books on Vietnam. J. William Fulbright's *The Arrogance of Power* (1967) contains shrewd and prescient essays, but Ernest Gruening and Herbert W. Beaser's *Vietnam Folly* (1968) is a pastiche. Senator Gale W. McGee makes a weak case for the administration in *The Responsibilities of World Power* (1968). Other defenses of our role in Vietnam are Frank N. Trager, *Why Vietnam?* (1966), Donald S. Zagoria, *Vietnam Triangle: Moscow, Peking, Hanoi* (1967), and United States Department of Defense, *Report on the War in Vietnam [as of 30 June 1968]* (1969).

Still more books on Vietnam include the accounts of incredible American atrocities by Seymour Hersh, *My Lai 4* (1970), and Richard Hammer, *One Morning in the War* (1970); see also Jonathan Schell, *The Military Half: An Account of the Destruction in Quang Ngai and Quang Tin* (1968). On peace efforts see David Kraslow and Stuart H. Loory, *The Secret Search for Peace in Vietnam* (1968), and Harlan Cleveland, *The Obligations of Power: American Diplomacy in Search for Peace* (1966). On international law and Vietnam there are Roger H. Hull and John C. Novogrod, *Law and Vietnam* (1968), and Richard A. Falk, ed., *The Vietnam War and International Law* (1967). See also Alice Lynd, ed., *We Won't Go: Personal Accounts of War Objectors* (1968); Dennis J. Duncanson, *Government and Revolution in Vietnam* (1968); Ralph Smith, *Viet-Nam and The West* (1968); General Vo Nguyen Giap, *Big Victory, Great Task* (1968); Thich Nhat-Hanh, *Vietnam: Lotus in a Sea of Fire* (1967); Piero Gheddo, *The Cross and the Bo-Tree* (1970); the Brookings report, *Vietnam after the War: Peacekeeping and Rehabilitation* (1968); and Robert Shaplen, *The Road from War* (1970).

VII. 1968 and After

The 1968 election is best covered in Lewis Chester et al., *An American Melodrama* (1969). On Nixon there is the fascinating study, *Nixon Agonistes* (1970), by Garry Wills. But see also Nixon's own *Six Crises* (1962); Earl Mazo and Stephen Hess, *Nixon: A Political Portrait* (1968); Ralph De Toledano, *One Man Alone: Richard M. Nixon* (1969); Joe McGinniss, *The Selling of the President 1968* (1969); and *The Resurrection of Richard Nixon* by Jules Witcover (1970). Kevin Phillips' *The Emerging Republican Majority* (1969) is very polemical.

On Hubert Humphrey there is the inadequate *Drugstore Liberal* (1968) by Robert Sherrill and Harry

Ernst, as well as Nelson W. Polsby, *The Citizen's Choice: Humphrey or Nixon* (1968), and Winthrop Griffith, *Humphrey* (1965). On Robert Kennedy, see Penn Kimball, *Bobby Kennedy and the New Politics* (1968); William V. Shannon, *The Heir Apparent* (1967); Douglas Ross, *Robert F. Kennedy* (1968); and Victor Lasky's *Robert F. Kennedy: The Myth and the Man* (1968). Arthur Schlesinger, Jr., is now preparing a badly needed book on Robert Kennedy. The Senator's own books are sparse in content: the best are *The Enemy Within* (1960) and *To Seek a Newer World* (1967). The McCarthy campaign inspired the Senator's own *The Year of the People* (1969), as well as three books written by supporters of various degrees of enthusiasm: Jeremy Larner, *Nobody Knows: Reflections on the McCarthy Campaign of 1968* (1970); Arthur Herzog, *McCarthy for President* (1969); and Ben Stavis, *We Were the Campaign* (1969).

VIII. The Radical Intuition

The *Report of the National Advisory Commission on Civil Disorders* (1968) is basic to an understanding of the violence of the sixties. Hugh Davis Graham and Ted Robert Gurr, *The History of Violence in America* (1969), contains many useful essays on violence and crime. Robert Conot, *Rivers of Blood, Years of Darkness* (1968), is a stunning account of the Watts riot. Tom Hayden, *Rebellion in Newark* (1967), discusses that incident. Garry Wills, *The Second Civil War: Arming for Armageddon* (1968), describes the armaments being assembled against urban blacks. Allen D. Grimshaw, ed., *Racial Violence in the United States* (1969), details the various explanations and even more numerous confusions over this mysterious subject. Richard Hofstadter and Michael Wallace, eds., *American Violence: A Documentary History* (1970), contains an important essay by Hofstadter on violence in American history.

The radicalism of the sixties has already found its first academic historian, James J. O'Brien, whose articles in *Radical America*, published serially in 1968, are part of a doctoral dissertation on the New Left. They form a useful summary of events and offer valuable bibliography, especially of articles in radical periodicals. Many of the sources of both the New Left and the cultural radicalism of the decade are to be uncovered in the vivid and extensive underground press. There are also several anthologies having use, including Paul Jacobs and Saul Landau, ed., *The New Radicals* (1966), which contains a useful chronology of the Left, and Mitchell Goodman, *The Movement toward a New America* (1970). The writings of Kenneth Keniston are brilliant and illuminating on youth and radicalism. See his *Young Radicals* (1968), and "Youth, Change, and Violence," *American Scholar* (1968), and "Youth: A New Stage of Life," *American Scholar* (1970). For a critical approach to the New Left see Irving Howe, ed., *Beyond the New Left* (1970); for a glowing one, the Newfield volume cited above. Michael Harrington, *Toward a Democratic Left* (1968), and Christopher Lasch, *The Agony of the American Left* (1969), are thoughtful books.

Stephen Spender's *The Year of the Young Rebels* (1969) is good on the international student movement. Edward E. Sampson, Harold A. Korn, et al., *Student Activism and Protest* (1970), is a valuable anthology of sociological studies of student activism. Seymour Lipset and Sheldon Wolin, eds., *The Berkeley Student Revolt* (1965), is the most complete collection of documents and analyses on the Berkeley incident of 1964. On Columbia in 1968 see Roger Kahn, *The Battle for Morningside Heights* (1970), and Jerry Avorn et al., *Up against the Ivy Wall* (1968). For sharp criticism of the students, see George Kennan, *Democracy and the Student Left* (1968).

Educational reform has been a major theme of the 1960s. James B. Conant in *The American High School Today* (1959), and *Slums and Suburbs* (1961), publicized this generation's crisis in American education. Some outstanding names among the new educational reformers are: Jerome S. Bruner, *The Process of Education* (1960) and *Toward a Theory of Instruction* (1966), spelled out a new progressivism which has been the subject of wide debate. John Holt, *How Children Fail* (1964), *How Children Learn* (1967), and *The Underachieving School* (1969), rallied educational reformers. Jonathan Kozol, *Death at an Early Age* (1967), graphically described the failings of urban schools, as had Charles Silberman, *Crisis in the Classroom* (1970). Clark Kerr, *The Uses of the University* (1963), is the classic description of the new "multiversity." David Riesman and Christopher Jencks, *The Academic Revolution* (1968), surveys and analyzes changes in higher education. Jacques Barzun, *The American University* (1968), defends the academy. James Ridgeway, *The*

Closed Corporation (1968), attacks it. Theodore Roszak, ed., *The Dissenting Academy* (1968), shows some of the discontent within.

The amorphous new culture of the sixties is best approached through the major books that have most influenced this sensibility. Herbert Marcuse's *An Essay on Liberation* (1969) is the best entree into the mind of this difficult thinker. Norman O. Brown, *Life against Death* (1959) and *Love's Body* (1966), and R. D. Laing, *The Politics of Experience* (1967), explore experiential moods. Frantz Fanon, *The Wretched of the Earth* (tr., 1965), has had a wide influence. Marshall McLuhan, *Understanding Media* (1964), has had major effect on thinking about the new sensibility. Various writings of Norman Mailer, especially "The White Negro," an essay reprinted in *Advertisements for Myself* (1959), have had wide effect. His *The Armies of the Night* (1968) has set standards for personal journalism and the display of sensibility that many imitate. Jerry Rubin's *Do It!* (1970) and Abbie Hoffman's *Woodstock Nation* (1969) have entertained many, outraged more, and influenced some.

An excellent book on the youth culture is Theodore Roszak's *The Making of a Counter Culture* (1969), although its emphasis on the youth culture as a revolt against technology slights several important themes in this movement and underestimates the relation between technology and the new sensibility. Charles Reich, *The Greening of America* (1970), is naive, exuberant, and often delightful. Philip Slater, *The Pursuit of Loneliness* (1970), presents an interesting sociological and psychological analysis of establishment culture and its cracking. Leslie Fiedler's "The New Mutants," *Partisan Review* (1965), is a valuable and in some ways prophetic statement. Warren Hinckle, "A Social History of the Hippies," *Ramparts* (1967), and Lewis Yablonsky, *The Hippie Trip* (1968), both present the scene. Tom Wolfe's *Electric Kool-Aid Acid Test* (1968), which views Ken Kesey's part of the new world, is a minor classic. Kesey's own *One Flew Over the Cuckoo's Nest* (1962) is a monument in fiction of the new sensibility, as in another way is Joseph Heller, *Catch-22* (1955). Rock music has spawned a number of books with differing emphases. Jerry Hopkins, *The Rock Story* (1970), is informative, and Hopkins' magazine, *Rolling Stone*, has become the standard rock world newsletter. Another part of this culture, the drug scene, is considered soberly in Erich Goode's anthology, *Marijuana* (1969), as well as in the Roszak and Yablonsky volumes mentioned above. For word from the source, see Timothy Leary, *The Politics of Ecstacy* (1968). Nonliterary sources, especially movies and music, are essential for any understanding of this new world.

Women's liberation is in part an offshoot of the new culture, although the one classic work, Betty Friedan's *The Feminine Mystique* (1963), has solid roots in the 1950s' suburbs. The newer movement is best approached through one of the several anthologies now available. Robin Morgan, ed., *Sisterhood Is Powerful* (1970), is among the best. Kate Millett, *Sexual Politics* (1970), has had a large vogue.

On religious changes in the 1960s, the works of Harvey Cox on Protestantism are perhaps the most stimulating. See *The Secular City* (1965) and Daniel J. Callahan, ed., *The Secular City Debate* (1966). The pseudonymous Xavier Rhynne's reports on Vatican II, published serially in the *New Yorker*, have had great impact on lay and clerical opinion in America of the changes in the Catholic Church. Developments in Judaism are regularly analyzed in the journal *Commentary*. Marshall Sklare's writings on the sociology of the American Jewish community are particularly useful.

Changing sexual mores have become a subject for considerable discussion. The volumes published by the Institute for Sexual Research (the Kinsey Institute) have been a basic source. See *Sexual Behavior in the Human Male* (1948), *Sexual Behavior in the Human Female* (1953), and *Sex Offenders* (1965). The work of William H. Masters and Virginia E. Johnson, *Human Sexual Response* (1966), as well as *Human Sexual Inadequacy* (1970), has had wide influence, especially on the women's rights movement. Robert J. Lifton, ed., *The Woman in America* (1965), contains several useful essays. On homosexuality see the persuasive Martin Hoffman, *The Gay World* (1968); on deviance generally, Ned Polsky, *Hustlers, Beats, and Others* (1967).

Summary views of the sixties by Richard Rovere and Benjamin DeMott appeared in *The New York Times Magazine*, December 14, 1969.

index